How to File for Divorce in Illinois

How to File for Divorce in Illinois

with forms

Darrell K. Seigler
Edward A. Haman
Attorneys at Law

Sphinx Publishing
A Division of Sourcebooks, Inc.
Naperville, IL • Clearwater, FL

Second Edition, 1999

Published by: **Sphinx® Publishing, A Division of Sourcebooks, Inc.®**

Naperville Office
P.O. Box 372
Naperville, Illinois 60566
(630) 961-3900
Fax: 630-961-2168

Clearwater Office
P.O. Box 25
Clearwater, Florida 33757
(727) 587-0999
Fax: 727-586-5088

Interior Design and Production: Shannon E. Harrington, Sourcebooks, Inc.

This publication is designed to provide accurate and authoritative information in regard to the subject matter covered. It is sold with the understanding that the publisher is not engaged in rendering legal, accounting, or other professional service. If legal advice or other expert assistance is required, the services of a competent professional person should be sought.

From a Declaration of Principles Jointly Adopted by a Committee of the American Bar Association and a Committee of Publishers and Associations

Library of Congress Cataloging-in-Publication Data

Seigler, Darrell K.,
How to file for divorce in Illinois : with forms / Darrell K. Seigler, Edward A. Haman. —2nd ed.
p. cm.
Includes index.
ISBN 1-57071-405-3 (pbk.)
1. Divorce suits—Illinois—Popular works. 2. Divorce—Law and legislation—Illinois—Popular works. I. Haman, Edward A. II. Title.
KFI1300.Z9S45 1998
346.7301'6—dc21

98-39102
CIP

Printed and bound in the United States of America.

Paperback — 10 9 8 7 6 5 4 3 2

CONTENTS

Using Self-Help Law Books

Whenever you shop for a product or service, you are faced with various levels of quality and price. In deciding what product or service to buy, you make a cost/value analysis on the basis of your willingness to pay and the quality you desire.

When buying a car, you decide whether you want transportation, comfort, status, or sex appeal. Accordingly, you decide among such choices as a Neon, a Lincoln, a Rolls Royce, or a Porsche. Before making a decision, you usually weigh the merits of each option against the cost.

When you get a headache, you can take a pain reliever (such as aspirin) or visit a medical specialist for a neurological examination. Given this choice, most people, of course, take a pain reliever, since it costs only pennies, whereas a medical examination costs hundreds of dollars and takes a lot of time. This is usually a logical choice because rarely is anything more than a pain reliever needed for a headache. But in some cases, a headache may indicate a brain tumor, and failing to see a specialist right away can result in complications. Should everyone with a headache go to a specialist? Of course not, but people treating their own illnesses must realize that they are betting on the basis of their cost/value analysis of the situation, they are taking the most logical option.

The same cost/value analysis must be made in deciding to do one's own legal work. Many legal situations are very straight forward, requiring a simple form and no complicated analysis. Anyone with a little intelligence and a book of instructions can handle the matter without outside help.

But there is always the chance that complications are involved that only an attorney would notice. To simplify the law into a book like this, several legal cases often must be condensed into a single sentence or paragraph. Otherwise, the book would be several hundred pages long and too complicated for most people. However, this simplification necessarily leaves out many details and nuances that would apply to special or unusual situations. Also, there are many ways to interpret most legal questions. Your case may come before a judge who disagrees with the analysis of our authors.

Therefore, in deciding to use a self-help law book and to do your own legal work, you must realize that you are making a cost/value analysis and deciding that the chance your case will not turn out to your satisfaction is outweighed by the money you will save in doing it yourself. Most people handling their own simple legal matters never have a problem, but occasionally people find that it ended up costing them more to have an attorney straighten out the situation than it would have if they had hired an attorney in the beginning. Keep this in mind while handling your case, and be sure to consult an attorney if you feel you might need further guidance.

INTRODUCTION

Going through a divorce is probably one of the most common, and most traumatic, encounters with the legal system. Paying a divorce lawyer can be one of the most expensive single bills to pay, and at a time when you are least likely to have extra funds. In a contested divorce case it is not uncommon for the parties to run up legal bills of over $10,000; and horror stories abound of lawyers charging substantial fees with little progress to show for it. This book is designed to enable you to obtain a divorce without hiring a lawyer. Even if you do hire a lawyer, this book will help you to work with him or her more effectively, which can also reduce the legal fee.

This is not a law school course, but a practical guide to get you through the system as easily as possible. Legal jargon has nearly been eliminated. For ease of understanding, this book uses the term *spouse* to refer to your husband or wife (whichever applies), and the terms *child* and *children* are used interchangeably.

Please keep in mind that different judges, and courts in different counties, may have their own particular (if not peculiar) procedures and ways of doing things. The court clerk's office can often tell you if they have any special forms or requirements. Court clerks cannot give legal advice, but they can tell you what their court or judges require.

The first two chapters of this book will give you an overview of the law and the legal system, and help you decide if you really want a divorce. Chapter 3 will help you decide if you want an attorney. The remaining chapters will show you what forms you need, how to fill out the forms, and what procedures to follow. You will also find two appendices in the back of the book. Appendix A contains selected portions of the Illinois law dealing with property division, alimony, and child support. Although these provisions are discussed in the book, it is sometimes helpful to read the law exactly as the legislature wrote it.

Finally, appendix B contains the forms you will complete. You will not need to use all of the forms. This book will tell you which forms you need, depending upon your situation.

Be sure to read "An Introduction to Legal Forms" in chapter 5 before you use any of the forms in this book.

1 Marriage "Ins and Outs"

Several years (or maybe only months) ago you decided to get married. This chapter will discuss, in a general way, what you got yourself into, and how you can get yourself out.

Marriage

Marriage is frequently referred to as a contract. It is a legal contract, and for many, it is also a religious contract. This book will deal only with the legal aspects. The wedding ceremony involves the bride and groom reciting certain vows, which are actually mutual promises about how they will treat each other. There are also legal papers signed, such as a marriage license and a marriage certificate. These formalities create certain rights and obligations for the husband and wife. Although the focus at the ceremony is on the emotional and romantic aspects of the relationship, the legal reality is that financial and property rights are being created. It is these financial and property rights and obligations which cannot be broken without a legal proceeding.

Marriage gives each of the parties certain rights in property, and creates certain obligations to support any children they have together (or adopt). Unfortunately, most people don't fully realize that these rights and obligations are being created until it comes time for a divorce.

Divorce

A divorce is the most common method of terminating or breaking the marriage contract. In Illinois, a divorce is officially called a *dissolution of marriage*. The laws, court rules, and legal papers all use this official term. In this book the terms *divorce* and *dissolution of marriage* are used interchangeably, and have the same meaning. In a divorce, the court declares the marriage contract broken, divides the parties' property and debts, decides if either party should receive alimony, and determines the custody, support, and visitation with respect to any children the parties may have. Traditionally, a divorce could only be granted under certain very specific circumstances, such as for adultery, or mental cruelty. Today, a divorce may be granted for various reasons, including general disagreement and poor relations. The wording used to describe the situation is an "irretrievable breakdown of the marriage." In Illinois, this ground, called *no-fault*, requires that the parties be separated at least six months and both choose to get divorced without waiting the required maximum separation time of two years (see chapter 7).

Invalidity of Marriage (Annulment)

The basic difference between a divorce and an annulment is that a divorce says "this marriage is broken," and an annulment says "there never was a marriage." In Illinois, an annulment is called a *declaration of invalidity of marriage*. An annulment is more difficult and often more complicated to prove, so it is not used very often. Annulments are only possible in a few circumstances, usually where one party deceived the other. If you decide that you want an annulment, you should consult an attorney. If you are seeking an annulment for religious reasons and need to go through a church procedure (rather than, or in addition to, a legal procedure), you should consult your priest or minister.

A divorce is generally easier to get than an annulment. How do you start it? Simply by asking. The Petition for Dissolution of Marriage (Form 7 or Form 11), is filed, stating the reasons, or grounds for asking for the divorce. That is all you need to do. However, in order to get an annulment you'll need to prove more. This proof will involve introducing various documents into evidence, and having other people come to testify at the court hearing.

Grounds for Annulment

Annulments can only be granted under one of the following circumstances:

1. If one of the parties was too young to get married. In Illinois, both parties must be at least eighteen years old to get married. (There are a few exceptions, such as where the under-age person has parental consent; but these exceptions only apply if the person is at least sixteen.)

2. If one of the parties is guilty of fraud. For example, where one party just got married in order to obtain property, or to have the right to inherit, from the other, with no intention of ever living together as husband and wife.

3. If one party was under duress when he or she got married. *Duress* means that the person was being threatened, or was under some kind of pressure, so that he or she did not get married voluntarily. This means real and not imagined force or threat.

4. If one party didn't have the mental capacity to get married. This means the person was suffering from mental illness or mental disability (such as being severely retarded), to such an extent that the person didn't understand he or she was getting married; or possibly didn't even understand the meaning of marriage.

5. If one party was already married to another person (bigamy). This might occur if one party married, mistakenly believing his divorce from his previous wife was final.

6. If the marriage is incestuous. Illinois law prohibits marriage between certain family members, such as brother and sister, aunt and nephew, or uncle and niece.

7. If one party can not consummate the marriage sexually and the other party did not know that at the time of marriage.

If your spouse wants to stop an annulment, there are several arguments he or she could make to further complicate the case. This area of the law is not as well defined as divorce. Annulments are much less common than divorces. The annulment procedure can be extremely complicated, and should not be attempted without consulting a lawyer.

Legal Separation

Illinois permits a legal separation. This procedure is used to divide the property and provide for child support in cases where the husband and wife live separately, but remain married. This was usually used to break the financial rights and obligations of a couple whose religion did not permit divorce. Some states refer to this procedure as "divorce from bed and board." Illinois requires proof of grounds, such as mental cruelty or irreconcilable differences, and all of the procedures of a divorce in order to get a judgment for legal separation. Legal separation is rare compared with divorce and the specifics are beyond the scope of this book.

Do You Really Want a Divorce?

Getting a divorce is one of the most emotionally stressful events in a person's life. Only the death of one's child or spouse creates more stress than a divorce. It will also have an impact on several aspects of your life, and can change your entire life-style. Before you begin the process of getting a divorce, you need to take some time to think about how it will affect your life. This section will help you examine these things, and offer alternatives in the event you want to try to save your relationship. Even if you feel absolutely sure that you want a divorce, you should still read this section so that you are prepared for what may follow.

Legal Divorce

In emotional terms, the legal aspect is the easiest part of divorce. It is simply the breaking of your matrimonial bonds; the termination of your marriage contract and partnership. The stress created here is that of going through a court system procedure, and having to deal with your spouse as you go through it. However, when compared to the other aspects of divorce, the legal divorce doesn't last as long. On the other hand, the legal divorce can be the most confrontational and emotionally explosive stage.

There are generally three matters to be resolved through the legal divorce:

1. The divorce of two people: Basically, this gives each the legal right to marry someone else.
2. The division of their property (and responsibility for debts).
3. The care and custody of their children.

Although it is theoretically possible for the legal divorce to be concluded within a few months, the legalities most often continue for years. This is mostly caused by the emotional aspects leading to battles over the children.

Social and Emotional Divorce

Divorce will have a tremendous impact on your social and emotional lives, which will continue long after you are legally divorced. These impacts include:

Lack of companionship. Even if your relationship is quite stormy, you are probably still accustomed to just having your spouse around. You may be able to temporarily put aside your problems, and at least somewhat support each other in times of mutual adversity (such as in dealing with a death in the family, the illness of your child, or hurricane damage to your home). You may also just feel a little more secure at night, just not being alone in the house. Even if your marriage is one of the most miserable, you may still notice at least a little emptiness, loneliness or solitude after the divorce. It may not be that you miss your spouse in particular, but just miss another person being around.

Grief. Divorce may be viewed as the death of a marriage, or maybe the funeral ceremony for the death of a marriage. And like the death of anyone or anything you've been close to, you will feel a sense of loss. This aspect can take you through all of the normal feelings associated with grief, such as guilt, anger, denial, and acceptance. You'll get angry and frustrated over the years you've "wasted." You'll feel guilty because you "failed to make the marriage work." You'll find yourself saying, "I can't believe this is happening to me." And, for months or even years, you'll spend a lot of time thinking about your marriage. It can be extremely difficult to put it all behind you, and to get on with your life.

The single's scene: dating. Your social life will change after divorce. If you want to avoid solitary evenings before the TV, you'll find yourself trying to get back into the "single's scene." This will probably involve a change in friends, as well as a change in life-style. First, you may find that your current friends, who are probably all married, no longer find you, as a single person, fit in with their circle. Gradually, or even quickly, you may find yourself dropped from their guest list. Now you've got to start making an effort to meet single people at work, going out on the town, and even dating! This experience can be very frightening, tiring, and frustrating after years of being away from this life-style. It can also be very difficult if you have custody of the kids. And the dating scene is (or at least should be) entirely changed with the ever-present threat of AIDS and other communicable diseases.

FINANCIAL DIVORCE

The financial aspect of divorce can be a very long and drastic adjustment. Divorce has a significant financial impact in just about every case. Many married couples are just able to make ends meet. After getting divorced there are suddenly two rent payments, two electric bills, etc. For the spouse without custody, there is also child support to be paid. For at least one spouse, and often for both, money becomes even tighter than it was before the divorce. Also, once you've divided your property, each of you will need to replace the items the other person got to keep. If she got the bedroom furniture and the pots and pans, he will need to buy his own. If he got the TV and the sofa, she will need to buy her own TV and sofa.

Children and Divorce

The effect upon your children, and your relationship with them, can often be the most painful and long-lasting aspect of divorce. Your family life will be permanently changed, as there will no longer be the "family." Even if you remarry, step-parents rarely bring back that same family feeling. Your relationship with your children may become strained as they work through their feelings of blame, guilt, disappointment, and anger. This strain may continue for many years. Your children may even need professional counseling. Also, as long as there is child support and visitation involved, you will be forced to have at least some contact with your ex-spouse.

Alternatives to Divorce

By the time you've purchased this book, and read this far, you have probably already decided that you want a divorce. However, if what you've just read and thought about has changed your mind, or made you want to make a last effort to save your marriage, there are a few things you can try. These are only very basic suggestions. Details, and other suggestions, can be offered by professional marriage counselors.

Talk to your spouse. Choose the right time (not when your spouse is trying to unwind after a day at work, or is trying to quiet a screaming baby), and talk about your problems. Try to establish a few ground rules for the discussion, such as:

- Talk about how you feel, instead of making accusations that may start an argument.
- Each person listens while the other speaks (no interrupting).
- Each person must say something that he or she likes about the other, and about the relationship.

As you talk you may want to discuss such things as where you'd like your relationship to go, how it has changed since you got married, and what can be done to bring you closer together.

Change your thinking. Many people get divorced because they won't change something about their outlook or their life-style. Then, once they get divorced, they find they've made that same change they resisted for so long.

For example, George and Wendy were unhappy in their marriage. They didn't seem to share the same life-style. George felt overburdened with responsibility, and bored. He wanted Wendy to be more independent and outgoing, to meet new people, to handle the household budget, and to go out with him more often. But Wendy was more shy and reserved, wasn't confident in her ability to find a job and succeed in the "business world," and preferred to stay at home. Wendy wanted George to give up some of his frequent nights "out with the guys," to help with the cooking and laundry, to stop leaving messes for her to clean up, and to stop bothering her about going out all the time. But neither would try change, and eventually all of the "little things" built up into a divorce.

After the divorce, Wendy was forced to get a job to support herself. Now she's made friends at work, she goes out with them two or three nights a week, she's successful and happy at her job, and she's quite competent at managing her own budget. George now has his own apartment, and has to cook his own meals (something he finds he enjoys), and do his own laundry. He's also found it necessary to clean up his own messes and keep the place neat, especially if he's going to entertain guests. George has even thought about inviting Wendy over for dinner and a quiet evening at his place. Wendy has been thinking about inviting George out for a drink after work with her friends.

Both George and Wendy have changed in exactly the way the other had wanted. It's just too bad they didn't make these changes before they got divorced! If you think some change may help, give it a try. You can always go back to a divorce if things don't work out.

Counseling. Counseling is not the same as giving advice. A counselor should not be telling you what to do. A counselor's job is to assist you in figuring out what you really want to do. A counselor's job is mostly to ask questions that will get you thinking.

Actually, just talking things out with your spouse is a form of self-counseling. The only problem is that it's difficult to remain objective and non-judgmental. You both need to be able to calmly analyze what the problems are, and discuss possible solutions.

Very few couples seem to be able to do this successfully, which is why there are professional marriage counselors. As with doctors and lawyers, good marriage counselors are best discovered by word of mouth. You may have friends who can direct you to someone who helped them. You can also check with your family doctor or your clergyman for a referral, or even check the telephone yellow pages under "Marriage and Family Counselors" or some similar category. You can see a counselor either alone or with your spouse. It may be a good idea to see a counselor even if you are going through with the divorce.

Another form of individual counseling is talking to a close friend. Just remember the difference between counseling and giving advice! Don't let your friend tell you what you should do.

Trial separation. Before going to the time, expense, and trouble of getting a divorce, you and your spouse may want to try just getting away from each other for awhile. This can be as simple as taking separate vacations, or as complex as actually separating into separate households for an indefinite period of time.

This may give each of you a chance to think about how you'll like living alone, how important or trivial your problems are, and how you really feel about each other.

2 THE LEGAL SYSTEM

This chapter will give you a general introduction to the legal system. There are things you need to know in order to obtain a divorce (or help your lawyer get the job done), and to get through any encounter with the legal system with minimum stress. These are some of the realities of our system. If you don't learn to accept these realities, you will experience much stress and frustration.

THEORY VS. REALITY

Our legal system is a system of rules. There are basically three types of rules:

1. *rules of law*: These provide the basic substance of the law, such as a law telling a judge how to go about dividing your property.
2. *rules of procedure*: These tell how matters are to be handled in the courts, such as requiring court papers to be in a certain form, or filed within a certain time.
3. *rules of evidence*: These require facts to be proven in a certain way.

The theory is that these rules allow each side to present evidence most favorable to that side, and an independent person or persons (the judge or jury) will be able to figure out the truth. Then certain legal principles will be applied to that "truth" which will give a fair resolution of the dispute between the parties. These legal principles are supposed to be relatively unchanging so that we can all know what will happen in any given situation and can plan our lives accordingly. This will provide order and predictability to our society. Any change in the legal principles is supposed to occur slowly, so that the expected behavior in our society is not confused from day-to-day. Unfortunately, the system does not really work this way. What follows are only some of the problems in the real legal system.

The System Is Not Perfect

Contrary to how it may seem, legal rules are not made just to complicate things and confuse everyone. They are attempts to make the system fair and just. They have been developed over several hundred years, and in most cases they do make sense. Unfortunately, our efforts to find fairness and justice have resulted in a complex set of rules. The legal system affects our lives in important ways, and it is not a game. However, it can be compared to a game in some ways. The rules are designed to apply to all people, in all cases. Sometimes the rules don't seem to give a fair result in a certain situation, but the rules are still followed. Just as a referee can make a bad call, so can a judge. There are also cases where one side wins by cheating.

Judges Don't Always Follow the Rules

This is a shocking discovery for many young lawyers. After spending three years in law school learning legal theory, and after spending countless hours preparing for a hearing and having all of the law on your side, you find that the judge isn't going to pay any attention to legal theories and the law. Many judges are going to make a decision simply on what they think seems fair under the circumstances. This concept is actually being taught in some law schools. Unfortunately, what seems fair to a particular judge may depend upon his personal ideas and philosophy. For example, there is nothing in the divorce laws that gives one parent priority in child custody; however, a majority of judges believe that a child is generally better off with its mother. All other things being equal, these judges will find a way to justify awarding custody to the mother.

The System Is Often Slow

Even lawyers get frustrated at how long it can take to get a case completed (especially if they don't get paid until it's done). Whatever your situation, things will take longer than you expect. Patience is required to get through the system with a minimum of stress. Don't let your impatience or frustration show. No matter what happens, keep calm, be courteous, and keep a positive attitude.

No Two Cases Are Alike

Just because your friend's case went a certain way doesn't mean yours will have the same result. The judge can make a difference, and more often the circumstances will make a difference. Just because your co-worker makes the same income as you and has the same number of children, you can't assume you will be ordered to pay the same amount of child support. There are usually other circumstances your co-worker doesn't tell you about, and possibly doesn't understand.

Half of the People Lose

Remember, there are two sides to every legal issue, and there is usually only one winner. Especially if you let the judge decide, don't expect to have every detail go your way. Often both parties leave the courthouse feeling that they lost.

Divorce Law and Procedure

This section will give you a general overview of the law and procedures involved in getting a divorce. To most people, including lawyers, the law appears very complicated and confusing. Fortunately, many areas of the law can be broken down into simple and logical steps. Divorce is one of those areas.

The Players

Law and the legal system are often compared to games, and just like games, it is important to know the players:

The judge. The judge has the power to decide whether you can get divorced, how your property will be divided, which of you will get custody of the children, and how much the other will pay for child support. The judge is the last person you want to make angry with you! In general, judges have large caseloads and like it best when your case can be concluded quickly and without hassle. This means that the more you and your spouse agree upon, and the more complete your paperwork, the better the judge will like it. Most likely, your only direct contact with the judge will be at the final hearing, which may last as little as five minutes. (See chapter 6 for more about how to deal with the judge).

The court clerk. The court clerk handles the files for all of the judges. The clerk's office is the central place where all of the court files are kept. The clerk files your court papers and keeps the official records of your divorce. Most people who work in the clerk's office are friendly and helpful. While they can't give you legal advice (such as telling you what to say in your court papers), they can help explain the system and the procedures (such as telling you what type of papers must be filed). The clerk has the power to accept or reject your papers, so you don't want to anger the clerk either. If the clerk tells you to change something in your papers, just change it. Don't argue or complain. Each judge will usually have an individual clerk that works with and handles his cases in the courtroom.

Lawyers. Lawyers serve as guides through the legal system. They try to guide their own client, while trying to confuse, manipulate, or outmaneuver their opponent. In dealing with your spouse's lawyer (if he or she has one) try to be polite. You won't get anywhere by being antagonistic. Generally the lawyer is just doing his job to get the best situation for his client. Some lawyers are truly nasty people. These lawyers simply can't be reasoned with, and you shouldn't try. If your spouse gets one of these lawyers, it is a good idea for you to get a lawyer also. Chapter 3 will provide more information to help you decide if you want a lawyer.

This book. This book will serve as your map through the legal system. In most cases, the dangers along the way are relatively small. If you start getting lost, or the dangers seem to be getting worse, you can always hire a lawyer to jump to your aid.

The Law

The law relating to divorce, as well as to any other area of law, comes from two sources. The first source is the Illinois Statutes, which are the laws passed by the Illinois Legislature. This book is designed so that you won't need to look up the law. However, a portion of this law, relating to property division, alimony, and child support, can be found in appendix A of this book.

The other source of law is the past decisions of the Illinois courts. These are much more difficult to locate and follow. For most situations the law is clearly spelled out in the statutes, and the past court decisions are not all that important. However, if you wish to learn more about how to find these court decision, see the section of this chapter on "Legal Research."

> ***Residency requirement:*** One basic law you need to be aware of is that either you or your spouse must live in Illinois for at least ninety days immediately before filing a petition with the court.

The law is really very simple in most divorce cases. You will need to show the following three things:

1. The reasons, or *grounds*, recognized by law for the divorce (for example, mental cruelty, irreconcilable differences/no-fault, etc.).
2. How your property should be divided between you and your spouse.
3. Who should have custody of your children and how they should be supported.

The Procedure

The basic uncontested divorce process may be viewed as a five-step process:

1. File court papers asking the judge to grant a divorce (which includes dividing your property and deciding the care of the children).

2. Notify your spouse that you are filing for divorce.
3. File papers explaining your financial situation, or what you and your spouse have agreed upon.
4. Obtain a hearing date.
5. Attend a hearing with the judge, and have the judge sign a judgment granting the divorce.

There is a simplified procedure that some people can use, which allows you to skip some of these steps. Now we'll look at these steps in a little more detail, and later chapters will tell you how to carry out these steps.

Petition for Dissolution of Marriage. This is simply a written request for the judge to grant you a divorce and divide your property. Forms for the Petition for Dissolution of Marriage are provided in appendix B of this book, and full instructions are also provided in later chapters. Once the Petition for Dissolution of Marriage is completed, it is taken to the court clerk to be filed.

Notifying your spouse. After you've prepared the Petition for Dissolution of Marriage you need to officially notify your spouse. Even though your spouse may already know that you are filing for divorce, you still need to have him or her officially notified. This is done by having a copy of your Petition for Dissolution of Marriage delivered to your spouse. This must be done in a certain way, which will be explained in detail later. (This step is eliminated in the simplified divorce procedure.)

Obtaining a hearing date. Once all of your paperwork has been filed, you need to set a date for a hearing. A hearing is simply a meeting with the judge so that he or she can give you a divorce. This is usually done by contacting the judge's secretary and asking for a hearing date. This can often be done over the telephone.

The hearing. Finally, you go to the hearing. The judge will review the papers you have submitted, and any additional information you have, and will make a decision about whether to grant the divorce, how your property should be divided, who should have custody of your children, and how the children are to be supported. If it applies to your situation, he may also decide whether alimony shall be paid. If you and your spouse agree on these matters, the judge will simply approve your agreement. In any procedure, contested or agreed, the judge will very likely hear testimony of the parties from the witness stand before making a decision or approving an agreement.

MEDIATION

The judge can order the husband and wife to mediation when they are having a difficult time reaching agreement on child custody and visitation. Also, marriage counseling can be ordered if the judge believes the marriage can be saved; however, this is an extremely rare situation. The judge can also direct the state Department of Children and Family Services or other agencies to conduct a study, and provide the judge with a custody recommendation.

LEGAL RESEARCH

This book has been designed so that you don't need to do research. However, if you need or want to find out more about the divorce law in Illinois, this section will give you some guidance.

ILLINOIS STATUTES

The main source of information on Illinois divorce law is the *Illinois Compiled Statutes*, which are the laws passed by the Illinois legislature. There are two sets of books which contain these laws. The first source is called *West's Smith-Hurd Illinois Compiled Statutes Annotated*, which also contains notes, or *annotations*, about how the law has been interpreted by the courts. For example, if you are looking for information about maintenance (alimony), you would find section 5/504. This would give you the exact wording of section 5/504 of the statute, which would be followed by summaries of court opinions explaining the maintenance statute. The second set is called *Illinois Compiled Statutes (State Bar Association Edition)*, which just contains the statutes. As the legislature meets each year and passes new laws, a new set of statute books is issued in even numbered years (1998, 2000, etc.), with periodic supplements. A set of statute books can usually be found at the public library, although check to be sure they have the most recent set. They usually aren't available until the beginning of the following year. Divorce laws are found in Chapter 750. You will find Chapter 750 is further divided into numbered "sections," such as "5/401," "5/402," etc.

In addition to the laws passed by the legislature, law is also made by the decisions of the judges in various cases each year. To find this *case law* you need to go to a law library. Each county has a law library connected with the court, so ask the court clerk where the law library is located. Also, law schools have libraries which may be open to the public. Don't be afraid to ask the librarian for assistance. They cannot give you legal advice, but they can tell you where the books are located. Case law may be found in the following:

ILLINOIS DIGEST

The *Illinois Digest* is a set of books which give short summaries of cases, and the place where you can find the court's full written opinion. The information in the digest is arranged alphabetically by subject. Find the chapter on "Divorce," then look for the headings of the subject you want.

NORTHEASTERN REPORTER

The *Northeastern Reporter* is where the appeals courts publish their written opinions on the cases they hear. There are two *series* of the *Northeastern Reporter*, the older cases being found in the *Northeastern Reporter* (abbreviated "N.E."), and newer cases being found in the *Northeastern Reporter 2d Series* ("N.E.2d"). For example, if the digest tells you that the case of *Smith v. Smith* is located at "149 N.E.2d 721," you can find the case by going to volume 149 of the *Northeastern Reporter 2d Series*, and turning to page 721.

ILLINOIS JURISPRUDENCE

Illinois Jurisprudence is a legal encyclopedia. You simply look up the subject you want ("Dissolution of Marriage"), in alphabetical order, and it gives you a summary of the law on that subject. It will also refer to specific court cases, which can then be found in the Northeastern Reporter.

ILLINOIS LAW AND PRACTICE

Illinois Law and Practice is a more expanded legal encyclopedia with case references.

OTHER SOURCES

Other books you may want to ask for at the law library are:

- *Family Law*, published by the Illinois Institute for Continuing Legal Education (IICLE).
- *Callaghan's Illinois Civil Practice Forms*.

For more help with legal research, see *Legal Research Made Easy*, by Suzan Herskowitz, which is available from your local bookstore or directly from Sphinx Publishing by calling 1-800-226-5291.

3 LAWYERS

Whether you need an attorney will depend upon many factors, such as how comfortable you feel handling the matter yourself, whether your situation is more complicated than usual, how much opposition you get from your spouse, and whether your spouse has an attorney. It may also be advisable to hire an attorney if you encounter a judge with a hostile attitude, or if your spouse gets a lawyer who wants to fight. There are no court appointed lawyers in divorce cases, so if you want an attorney you will have to hire one.

A very general rule is that you should consider hiring an attorney whenever you reach a point where you no longer feel comfortable representing yourself. This point will vary greatly with each person, so there is no easy way to be more definite. You should get an attorney if your spouse is in the military and is unwilling to either file a Response to Petition for Dissolution of Marriage (Form 13 in appendix B) or sign a settlement agreement (Form 10 or Form 19), or use the simplified divorce procedure described in chapter 6.

Rather than asking if you *need* a lawyer, a more appropriate question may be: "Do you *want* a lawyer?" The next section will discuss some of the "pros" and "cons" of hiring a lawyer, and some of the things you may want to consider in making this decision.

Do You Want a Lawyer?

One of the first questions you will want to consider, and most likely the reason you are reading this book, is: How much will an attorney cost? Attorneys come in all ages, shapes, sizes, sexes, racial and ethnic groups—and price ranges. For a very rough estimate, you can expect an attorney to charge anywhere from $150 to $1,000 for an uncontested divorce, and from $800 and up for a contested divorce. Lawyers usually charge an hourly rate for contested divorces, ranging from about $75 to $300 per hour. Most new (and therefore less expensive) attorneys would be quite capable of handling a simple divorce, but if your situation became more complicated, you would probably prefer a more experienced lawyer.

Some Advantages to Hiring a Lawyer

Some advantages to hiring a lawyer include:

- ☛ Judges and other attorneys may take you more seriously. Most judges prefer both parties to have attorneys. They feel this helps the case move in a more orderly fashion, because both sides will know the procedures and relevant issues. Persons representing themselves very often waste a lot of time on matters which have absolutely no bearing on the outcome of the case.
- ☛ A lawyer will serve as a "buffer" between you and your spouse. This can lead to a quicker passage through the system, by reducing the chance for emotions to take control and confuse the issues.
- ☛ Attorneys prefer to deal with other attorneys, for the same reasons listed above. However, if you become familiar with this book, and conduct yourself in a calm and proper manner, you should have no trouble. (Proper courtroom manners will be discussed in chapter 5.)
- ☛ You can let your lawyer worry about all of the details. By having an attorney you need only become generally familiar with the

contents of this book, as it will be your attorney's job to file the proper papers in the correct form, and to deal with the court clerks, the judge, the process server, your spouse, and your spouse's attorney.

- Lawyers provide professional assistance with problems. In the event your case is complicated, or suddenly becomes complicated, it is an advantage to have an attorney who is familiar with your case. It can also be comforting to have a lawyer to turn to for advice, and to get your questions answered.

Some Advantages to Representing Yourself

Some advantages to representing yourself include:

- You save the cost of a lawyer.
- Sometimes judges feel more sympathetic toward a person not represented by an attorney. Sometimes this results in the unrepresented person being allowed a certain amount of leeway with the procedure rules.
- The procedure may be faster. Two of the most frequent complaints about lawyers received by the bar association involve delay in completing the case, and failure to return phone calls. Most lawyers have a heavy caseload, which sometimes results in cases being neglected for various periods of time. If you are following the progress of your own case you'll be able to push it along the system diligently.
- Selecting any attorney is not easy. As the next section shows, it is hard to know whether you are selecting an attorney that will make you happy.

Middle Ground

As an alternative to being fully represented by a lawyer, you may want to look for an attorney who will be willing to accept an hourly fee to answer your questions and give you help as you need it. This way you will save some legal costs, but still get some professional assistance.

Selecting a Lawyer

This is a two-step process. First you need to decide which attorney to make an appointment with, then you need to decide if you want to hire that attorney.

Finding Lawyers

The following are suggestions for how to go about finding two or three lawyers for consideration.

- Ask a friend. A common, and frequently the best, way to find a lawyer is to ask someone you know to recommend one to you. This is especially helpful if the lawyer represented your friend in a divorce, or other family law matter.
- Check with a lawyer referral service. You can find a referral service by looking in the yellow pages phone directory under "Attorney Referral Services" or "Attorneys." This is a service, usually operated by a bar association, which is designed to match a client with an attorney handling cases in the area of law the client needs. The referral service does not guarantee the quality of work, nor the level of experience or ability, of the attorney. Finding a lawyer this way will at least connect you with one who is interested in divorce and family law matters, and probably has some experience in this area.
- Check the yellow pages. Check under the heading for "Attorneys" in the yellow pages phone directory. Many lawyers and law firms place display ads indicating their areas of practice and educational backgrounds. Look for firms or lawyers indicating they practice in areas such as "divorce," "family law," or "domestic relations."
- Ask another lawyer. If you have used the services of an attorney in the past for some other matter (for example, a real estate closing, traffic ticket, or a will), you may want to call and ask if he or she could refer you to an attorney whose ability in the area of family law is respected.

Evaluating a Lawyer

From your search you should select three to five lawyers worthy of further consideration. Your first step will be to call each attorney's office, explain that you are interested in seeking a divorce, and ask the following questions:

- Does the attorney (or firm) handle this type of matter?
- How much can you expect it to cost? (Don't expect to get a definite answer, and you may not be able to get any answer until you discuss your case with the lawyer. Either at this point, or when you meet with the lawyer, you should be able to get and idea of what to expect for a simple case, and what variables will increase the cost.)
- How soon can you get an appointment?

If you like the answers you get, ask if you can speak to the attorney. Some offices will permit this, but others will require you to make an appointment. Make the appointment if that is what is required. Once you get in contact with the attorney (either on the phone or at the appointment), ask the following questions:

- How much will it cost?
- How will the fee be paid?
- How long has the attorney been in practice?
- How long has the attorney been in practice in Illinois?
- What percentage of the attorney's cases involve divorce cases or other family law matters? (Don't expect an exact answer, but you should get a rough estimate that is at least twenty percent.)
- How long will it take? (Don't expect an exact answer, but the attorney should be able to give you an average range and discuss things which may make a difference.)

If you get acceptable answers to these questions, it's time to ask yourself the following questions about the lawyer:

- Do you feel comfortable talking to the lawyer?
- Is the lawyer friendly toward you?
- Does the lawyer seem confident in himself or herself?
- Does the lawyer seem to be straight-forward with you, and able to explain things so that you understand?

If you get satisfactory answers to all of these questions you'll probably be satisfied with your lawyer. Most clients are happiest with an attorney that makes them feel comfortable.

Working with a Lawyer

In general, you will work best with your attorney if you keep an open, honest and friendly attitude. You should also consider the following suggestions.

Ask Questions

If you want to know something or if you don't understand something, ask your attorney. If you don't understand the answer, tell your attorney and ask him or her to explain it again. There are many points of law that many lawyers don't fully understand, so you shouldn't be embarrassed to ask questions. Many people who say they had a bad experience with a lawyer either didn't ask enough questions, or had a lawyer who wouldn't take the time to explain things to them. If your lawyer isn't taking the time to explain what he's doing, it may be time to look for a new lawyer.

Be Thorough

Give your lawyer complete information. Anything you tell your attorney is confidential, so don't hold back. An attorney can lose his license to practice if he reveals information without your permission. Tell your lawyer everything, even if it doesn't seem important to you. There are many things that seem unimportant to a non-attorney, but can change the outcome of a case. Also, don't hold back because you are afraid it will hurt your case. It will definitely hurt your case if your lawyer doesn't find out about it until he hears it in court from your spouse's attorney! But if he knows in advance, he can plan to eliminate or reduce damage to your case.

Accept Reality Listen to what your lawyer tells you about the law and the system. It won't do you any good to argue because the law or the system doesn't work the way you think it should. For example, if your lawyer tells you that the judge can't hear your case for two weeks, don't try demanding that he set a hearing tomorrow. By refusing to accept reality, you are only setting yourself up for disappointment. Remember: It's not your attorney's fault that the system isn't perfect, or that the law doesn't say what you'd like it to say.

Patience Be patient with the system (which is often slow as we discussed earlier), as well as with your attorney. Don't expect your lawyer to return your phone call within an hour. He may not be able to return it the same day either. Most lawyers are very busy, and over-worked. It is rare that an attorney can maintain a full case load and still make each client feel as if he is the only client.

Talk to the Secretary Your lawyer's secretary can be a valuable source of information. So be friendly and get to know the secretary. Often he or she will be able to answer your questions, and you won't get a bill for the time you talk to the secretary.

Dealing with Your Spouse Let your attorney deal with your spouse. It is your lawyer's job to communicate with your spouse, or with your spouse's lawyer. Let your lawyer do his or her job. Many lawyers have had clients lose or damage their cases when the client decides to say or do something on their own.

Promptness Be on time to appointments with your lawyer, and to court hearings.

Keep Your Case Moving Many lawyers operate on the old principle of the squeaking wheel gets the oil. Work on a case tends to get put off until a deadline is near, an emergency develops, or the client calls. Many lawyers take more cases than can be effectively handled in order to make the income they desire. Your task is to become a squeaking wheel that doesn't squeak too much. Whenever you talk to your lawyer ask the following questions:

- What is the next step?
- When do you expect it to be done?
- When should I talk to you next?

If you don't hear from the lawyer when you expect, call him the following day. Don't remind him that he didn't call; just ask how things are going.

How to Save Money

Of course you don't want to spend unnecessary money for an attorney. Here are a few things you can do to avoid excess legal fees:

- Don't make unnecessary phone calls to your lawyer.
- Give information to the secretary whenever possible.
- Direct your question to the secretary first. Your question will be referred to the attorney if the secretary can't answer it.
- Plan your phone calls so you can get to the point, and take less of your attorney's time.
- Do some of the "leg work" yourself. Pick up and deliver papers yourself, for example. Ask your attorney what you can do to assist with your case.
- Be prepared for appointments. Have all related papers with you, plan your visit to get to the point, and make an outline of what you want to discuss and what questions you want to ask.

Payment

Pay your attorney bill when it's due. No client gets prompt attention like a client who pays his lawyer on time. However, you are entitled to an itemized bill, showing what the attorney did and how much time it took. Many attorneys will have you sign an agreement stating how you will be charged, what is included in the hourly fee, and what is extra. Review your bill carefully. There are numerous stories of people paying an attorney $500 or $1,000 in advance, only to have the attorney make a few phone calls to the spouse's lawyer, then ask for more money. If your attorney asks for $500 or $1,000 in advance, you should be sure that you and the lawyer agree on what is to be done for this fee. For $500 you should at least expect to have a petition prepared, filed with the court, and served on your spouse (although the filing and service fees will probably be extra).

Firing Your Lawyer

If you find that you can no longer work with your lawyer, it is time to either go it alone or get a new attorney. You will need to send your lawyer a letter stating that you no longer desire his or her services, and are discharging him or her from your case. Also state that you will be coming by his or her office to pick up your file. The attorney does not have to give you his or her own notes or other work in progress, but you are entitled to the essential contents of your file (such as copies of papers already filed or prepared and billed for, and any documents you provided). If the attorney refuses to give your file to you, contact the state bar association about filing a complaint. Of course, you will need to settle any remaining fees charged. Then the attorney is required to turn over your file.

4 Evaluating Your Situation

The following things should be done or considered before you begin the divorce process.

Your Spouse

First, you need to evaluate your situation with respect to your spouse. Have you both already agreed to get a divorce? If not, what kind of reaction do you expect from him or her? Your expected reaction can determine how you proceed. If he or she reacts in a rational manner, you can probably use the simplified or uncontested procedure. But if you expect an extremely emotional, and possibly violent, reaction, you will need to take steps to protect yourself, your children, and your property; and will have to start out expecting to use the contested procedure.

You were warned on the back cover of this book not to let your spouse find this book, and it was for a very good reason. Unless you and your spouse have already decided together to get a divorce, you don't want your spouse to know you are thinking about filing for divorce. This is a defense tactic, although it may not seem that way at first.

If your spouse thinks you are planning a divorce, he or she may do things to prevent you from getting a fair result. These things include withdrawing money from bank accounts, hiding information about income, and hiding assets. So don't let on until you've collected all of the information you will need and are about to file with the court, or until you are prepared to protect yourself from violence, if necessary.

> ***Caution:*** Tactics such as withdrawing all money from bank accounts and hiding assets are dangerous. If you try any of these things you risk looking like the "bad guy" before the judge. This can result in anything from having disputed matters resolved in your spouse's favor, to being ordered to produce the assets (or be jailed for contempt of court). If funds are short and you decide to leave the marital home, take half the account.

Theoretically, the system would prefer you to keep evidence of the assets (such as photographs, sales receipts, or bank statements), to present to the judge if your spouse hides them. Then your spouse will be the bad guy and risk being jailed. However, once your spouse has taken assets, and hidden them, or sold them and spent the money, even a contempt order may not get the money or assets back. If you determine that you need to get the assets in order to keep your spouse from hiding or disposing of them, be sure you keep them in a safe place, and disclose them on your Financial Affidavit (Form 12). Do not dispose of them. If your spouse claims you took them, you can explain to the judge why you were afraid that your spouse would dispose of them and that you merely got them out of his or her reach.

Gathering Information

It is extremely important that you collect all of the financial information you can get. This information should include originals or copies of the following:

1. your most recent income tax return (and your spouse's if you filed separately).
2. the most recent W-2 tax forms for yourself and your spouse.
3. any other income reporting papers (such as interest, stock dividends, etc.).
4. your spouse's most recent pay stub, hopefully showing year-to-date earnings (otherwise try to get copies of all pay stubs since the beginning of the year).
5. deeds to all real estate; and titles to cars, boats, or other vehicles.
6. your and your spouse's will.
7. life insurance policies.
8. stocks, bonds, or other investment papers.
9. pension or retirement fund papers and statements.
10. health insurance card and papers.
11. bank account or credit union statements.
12. your spouse's social security number, and driver's license number.
13. names, addresses, and phone numbers of your spouse's employer, close friends, and family members.
14. credit card statements, mortgage documents, and other credit and debt papers.
15. a list of vehicles, furniture, appliances, tools, etc., owned by you and your spouse. (See the next section in this chapter on "Property and Debts" for forms and a detailed discussion of what to include.)
16. copies of bills or receipts for recurring, regular expenses, such as electric, gas or other utilities, car insurance, etc.

17. copies of bills, receipts, insurance forms, or medical records for any unusual medical expenses (including for recurring or continuous medical conditions) for yourself, your spouse, or your children.

18. any other papers showing what you and your spouse earn, own or owe.

Make copies of as many of these papers as possible, and keep them in a safe and private place (where your spouse won't find them). Try to make copies of new papers as they come in, especially as you get close to filing court papers, and as you get close to a court hearing.

Property and Debts

Property

This section is designed to help you get a rough idea of where things stand regarding the division of your property, and to prepare you for completing the court papers you will need to file. The following sections will deal with the questions of your debts, child support, custody, and visitation. If you are still not sure whether you want a divorce, these sections may help you to decide.

This section basically assists you in completing the Property Inventory (Form 1). First, you will need to understand how property is divided into marital and nonmarital property. Trying to determine how to divide assets and debts can be difficult. Under the Illinois *equitable distribution* law, assets and debts are separated into two categories: *marital* (meaning it is both yours and your spouse's), and *nonmarital* (meaning it is yours or your spouse's alone). (Also see Section 5/503 of the Illinois Statutes in appendix A.) In making this distinction the following rules apply:

1. If the asset or debt was acquired after the date you were married, it is presumed to be a marital asset of debt. It is up to you or your spouse to prove otherwise.

2. In order to be a nonmarital asset or debt, it must have been acquired before the date of your marriage. Also, it is nonmarital if you acquired it through a gift or inheritance (as long as it wasn't a gift from your spouse), and this includes income from nonmarital property. (Example: rent you receive from an investment property you had before you got married.) If you exchange one of these assets of debts after your marriage, it is still nonmarital. (Example: you had a $6,000 car before you got married. After the marriage, you traded it for a different $6,000 car.) Finally, you and your spouse may have signed a written agreement that certain assets and debts are to be considered marital or nonmarital, called a *prenuptial agreement, antenuptial agreement*, or *premarital agreement*.

3. Marital assets and debts are those that were acquired during your marriage, even if they were acquired by you or your spouse individually. This also includes the increase in value of a nonmarital asset during the marriage, or due to the use of marital funds to pay for or improve the property. All rights accrued during the marriage in pension, retirement, profit-sharing, insurance, and similar plans are marital assets. It is also possible for one spouse to make a gift of nonmarital property to the other spouse, thereby making it marital property. Even mixing nonmarital with marital property can make it all marital.

4. Real estate that is in both names is considered marital property, and it's up to the spouse claiming otherwise to prove it.

5. Finally, whether an asset of debt is marital or nonmarital, and the value of any asset is determined as of the date of the final judgement of divorce.

6. If property was acquired during the marriage, with marital funds or income, the names on the title or deed to real estate do not matter. The property is marital and will be divided.

The Property Inventory (Form 1) and Debt Inventory (Form 2), and the instructions that follow, call for a rather specific, detailed listing of property and debt items. You will notice that the Property Inventory (Form 1) is divided into nine columns, designated as follows:

Column (1): You will check the box in this column if that piece of property is nonmarital property. This is property that either you or your spouse acquired before you were married, or which were given to you or your spouse separately, or which were inherited by you or your spouse separately. (See appendix A, Section 5/503 of Illinois Compiled Statutes on "Disposition of Property," for a detailed explanation of marital and nonmarital assets and liabilities.)

Column (2): In this column you will describe the property. A discussion regarding what information should go in this column will follow.

Column (3): This column is used to write in the serial number, account number, or other number which will help clearly identify that piece of property.

Column (4): This is for the current market value of the property.

Column (5): This will show how much money is owed on the property, if any.

Column (6): Subtract the "Balance Owed" from the "Value." This will show how much the property is worth to you (your "Equity").

Column (7): This column will show the current legal owner of the property. (H) designates the husband, (W) the wife, and (J) is for jointly owned property (in both of your names).

Column (8): This column will be checked for those pieces of property you expect the husband will keep.

Column (9): This column is for the property you expect the wife will keep.

Use columns (1) through (7) to list your property, including the following:

Cash. List the name of the bank, credit union, etc., and the account number, for each account. This includes savings and checking accounts, and certificates of deposit (CDs). The balance of each account should be listed in the columns entitled "Value" and "Equity" (Leave the "Balance Owed" column blank.) Make copies of the most recent bank statements for each account.

Stocks and bonds. All stocks, bonds or other "paper investments" should be listed. Write down the number of shares and the name of the company or other organization that issued them. Also copy any notation such as "common" or "preferred" stock or shares. This information can be obtained from the stock certificate itself, or from a statement from the stock broker. Make a copy of the certificate or the statement.

Real estate. List each piece of property you and your spouse own. The description might include a street address for the property, a subdivision name and lot number, or anything which lets you know to what piece of property you are referring. There probably won't be an ID number, although you might use the county's tax number. Real estate (or any other property) may be in both of your names (joint), in your spouse's name alone, or in your name alone. The only way to know for sure is to look at the deed to the property. (If you can't find a copy of the deed, try to find mortgage papers or payment coupons, home-owners insurance papers, or a property tax assessment notice.) The owners of property are usually referred to on the deed as the *grantees*. In assigning a value to the property, consider the market value, which is how much you could probably get if you sold it. This might be what similar houses in your neighborhood have sold for recently. You might also consider how much you paid for the property, or for how much the property is insured. *Do not* use the tax assessment value, as this is usually considerably lower than the market value.

Vehicles. This category includes cars, trucks, motor homes, recreational vehicles (RVs), motorcycles, boats, trailers, airplanes, and any other means of transportation for which the State requires a title and registration. Your description should include the following information (which can usually be found on the title or on the vehicle itself):

- year it was made.
- make: The name of the manufacturer, such as "Ford," "Honda," "Chris Craft," etc.
- model: You know it's a Ford, but is it a Mustang, an LTD, or an Aerostar: The model may be a name, a number, a series of letters, or a combination of these.
- serial number: This is most likely found on the vehicle, as well as on the title or registration.

Make a copy of the title or registration. Regarding a value, you can go to the public library and ask to look at the blue book for cars, trucks, etc. A *blue book* (which may actually be yellow, black or any other color) gives the average values for used vehicles. Your librarian can help you find what you need. Another source is to look in the classified advertising section of a newspaper to see how similar vehicles are priced. You might also try calling a dealer to see if he can give you a rough idea of the value. Be sure you take into consideration the condition of the vehicle.

Furniture. List all furniture as specifically as possible. You should include the type of piece (such as sofa, coffee table, etc.), the color, and if you know it, the manufacturer, line name, or the style. Furniture usually won't have a serial number, although if you find one be sure to write it on the list. Just estimate a value, unless you know what it's worth.

Appliances, electronic equipment, yard machines, etc. This category includes such things as refrigerators, lawn mowers, and power tools. Again, estimate a value, unless you are familiar enough with them to simply know what they are worth. There are too many different makes, models, accessories, and age factors to be able to figure out a value otherwise. These items will probably have a make, model, and serial number on them. You may have to look on the back, bottom, or other hidden place for the serial number, but try to find it.

Jewelry and other valuables. You don't need to list inexpensive, or costume jewelry. You can plan on keeping your own personal watches, rings, etc. However, if you own an expensive piece you should include it in your list, along with an estimated value. Be sure to include silverware, original art, gold, coin collections, etc. Again, be as detailed and specific as possible.

Life insurance with cash surrender value. This is any life insurance policy that you may cash in or borrow against, and therefore has value. If you can't find a cash surrender value in the papers you have, you can call the insurance company and ask.

Other "big ticket" items. This is simply a general reference to anything of significant value that doesn't fit in one of the categories already discussed. Examples might be a portable spa, an above-ground swimming pool, golf clubs, guns, pool tables, camping or fishing equipment, or farm animals or machinery.

Pensions and military benefits. The division of pensions, and military and retirement benefits, can be a complicated matter. Whenever these types of benefits are involved, you will need to consult an attorney or a CPA to determine the value of the benefits and how they should be divided. Be sure to read the section in chapter 11 on pension plans.

What not to list. You will not need to list your clothing and other personal effects. Pots, pans, dishes, and cooking utensils ordinarily do not need to be listed, unless they have some unusually high value.

Once you have completed your list, go back through it and try to determine who should have each item. The ideal situation is for both you and your spouse to go through the list together, and divide things fairly. However, if this is not possible, you will need to offer a reasonable settlement to the judge. Consider each item, and make a check-mark in either column (8) or (9) to designate whether that item should go to the husband or wife. You may make the following assumptions:

- Your nonmarital property will go to you.
- Your spouse's nonmarital property will go to your spouse.
- You should get the items that only you use.
- Your spouse should get the items only used by your spouse.
- The remaining items should be divided, evening out the total value of all the marital property, and taking into consideration who would really want that item.

To somewhat equally divide your property (we're only talking about marital property here), you first need to know the total value of your property. First of all, do not count the value of the nonmarital items. Add the remaining amounts in the "Equity" column of Form 1, which will give you an approximate value of all marital property.

When it comes time for the hearing, you and your spouse may be arguing over some or all of the items on your list. This is when you'll be glad that you made copies of the documents relating to the property on your list. Arguments over the value of property may need to be resolved by hiring appraisers to set a value; however, you'll have to pay the appraiser a fee. Dividing your property will be discussed further in later chapters. (See chapter 8 for information on dividing property in contested cases.)

Debts This section relates to the Debt Inventory (Form 2), which will list your debts. Although there are cases where, for example, the wife gets a car but the husband is ordered to make the payments, generally whoever gets the property also gets the debt owed on that property. This seems to be a fair arrangement in most cases. On Form 2 you will list each debt owed by you or your spouse. As with nonmarital property, there is also nonmarital debt. This is any debt incurred before you were married, that is yours alone. Form 2 contains a column for "N-M" debts, which should be checked for each nonmarital debt. You will be responsible for your nonmarital debts, and your spouse will be responsible for his or hers.

To complete the Debt Inventory (Form 2), list each debt as follows:

Column (1):	Check if this is a nonmarital debt. (See appendix A, Section 5/503 of the Illinois Compiled Statutes, for a detailed explanation of marital and nonmarital assets and debts.)
Column (2):	Write in the name and address of the creditor (the bank, company, or person the debt is owed to).
Column (3):	Write in the account, loan, or mortgage number.
Column (4):	Write in any notes to help identify what the loan was for (such as Christmas gifts, vacation, etc.).
Column (5):	Write in the amount of the monthly payment.
Column (6):	Write in the balance still owed on the loan.
Column (7):	Write in the date (approximately) when the loan was made.
Column (8):	Note whether the account is in the husband's name (H), the wife's name (W), or jointly in both names (J).
Columns (9) and (10):	These columns note who will be responsible for the debt after the divorce. As with your property, each of you will keep your nonmarital debts, and the remainder should be divided taking into consideration who will keep the property the loan was for and equally dividing the debt. (See chapter 8 for information on dividing debts in contested cases.)

CHILD CUSTODY AND VISITATION

As with everything else in divorce, things are ideal when both parties can agree on the question of custody of the children. Generally the judge will accept any agreement you reach, provided it doesn't appear that your agreement will cause harm to your children.With respect to child custody, Illinois law uses a single key question in deciding all issues, including visitation: What is in the best interest of the children? The judge will look at the factors listed in appendix A, Section 5/602, in determining the best interest of the children. No single factor is more important and all factors are looked at very closely.

The old preference for mothers having custody of a young child is gone from the law itself. However, you will find that most judges are from the old school of thought on this subject and believe that (all things being equal) a young child is better off with the mother. Because of these policies in the law of equal treatment the judge may go to great lengths to find that all things are not equal, so as to justify his decision to award custody to the mother. It happens day after day throughout the state, and you may have to deal with this reality.

The Illinois law also provides that, unless good reason exists not to, the court must consider either party's request for what is commonly known as *joint custody*. While it is a great idea in its concept, it is usually not a practical one. Few parents can put aside their anger at each other to agree on what is best for their child. Joint custody merely leads to more fighting. And even if joint custody is ordered, a child can only have one primary residence. So the judge may still decide which parent the child will mainly live with, as well as how decisions regarding such things as education, and medical and dental care will be made. Many uncontested divorces do include joint custody, with the rules set down in a *joint parenting agreement*.

If you and your spouse cannot agree on how these matters will be handled, you will be leaving this important decision to the judge. The judge cannot possibly know your child as well as you and your spouse, so doesn't it make sense for you to work this out yourselves? Otherwise you are leaving the decision to a stranger.

Custody Factors

If the judge must decide the question, he or she will consider the following factors:

- the wishes of the parents are to custody.
- the wishes of the child as to his custodian.
- the interaction and interrelationship of the child with his parents, siblings, and other significant persons.
- the child's adjustment to his current home, school, and community.
- the mental and physical health of the parents and children involved.
- any physical violence or threat of physical violence by one of the parties, whether directed against the child or against another person.
- any occurrence of ongoing abuse, including physical and emotional abuse, defined by the Illinois Domestic Violence Act, whether directed against the child or against another person.
- the willingness and the ability of each parent to facilitate and encourage a close and continuing relationship between the other parent and the child.
- any other fact that the judge properly decides is relevant.

It is difficult to predict the outcome of a custody battle. There are too many factors and individual circumstances to make such a guess. The only exception is where one parent is clearly unfit and the other can prove it. Drug abuse is probably the most common charge against a spouse, but unless there has been an arrest and conviction it is difficult to prove to a judge. In general, don't charge your spouse with being unfit unless you can prove it. Judges are not impressed with unfounded allegations, and they can do more harm that good.

If your children are older (not infants), it may be a good idea to seriously consider their preference for with whom they would like to live. Your "fairness" and respect for their wishes may benefit you in the long run. Just be sure that you keep in close contact with them and visit them often. Also, be aware that some courts may require you to take classes on the effects of divorce on children.

Child Support

Once again, the judge will probably go along with any agreement you and your spouse reach, as long as he is satisfied that the child will be adequately taken care of. The following information and the child support guidelines in the statutes (Section 5/505 in appendix A), will help you get an idea of the proper amount of child support. Later, after you have more accurate income information, you will complete the Financial Affidavit (Form 12) to file with the court clerk.

How Child Support Is Determined

Generally there are two factors used to determine the proper amount of support to be paid: (1) the needs of the child, and (2) the financial ability of each parent to meet those needs. Illinois has simplified this procedure by establishing a minimum amount guidelines (Section 5/505 in appendix A). The following steps are used in determining the proper amount of support:

1. You and your spouse each provide proof of your gross income.
2. Taxes and other deductions are allowed to determine the *net income* for each of you.
3. Your net incomes are added together to arrive at your *combined income.*

4. The net income of the parent without custody is multiplied by the stated percentage based on the number of children to be supported.

5. That amount can be increased or decreased by the judge if he or she states the reason for doing so. In the great majority of cases, the percentage guidelines are closely followed.

INCOME DETERMINATION

Gross income. The first thing you will need to do is determine your *gross income* and list it on your Financial Affidavit (Form 12). This is basically your income before any deductions for taxes, social security, etc. The following money sources are considered part of gross income:

- ☛ salary or wages.
- ☛ overtime, commissions, bonuses, allowances, tips, etc.
- ☛ business income from self-employment, partnerships, corporations, and independent contracts (gross receipts, minus ordinary and necessary expenses).
- ☛ disability benefits.
- ☛ worker's compensation.
- ☛ unemployment compensation.
- ☛ pension, retirement, or annuity payments.
- ☛ social security benefits.
- ☛ alimony received from a previous marriage.
- ☛ interest and dividends.
- ☛ rental income (gross receipts, minus ordinary and necessary expenses—but not depreciation).
- ☛ income from royalties, trusts, or estates.

- reimbursed expenses to the extent they reduce living expenses (such as a rent allowance, or the value of an apartment provided by your employer).
- gains derived from dealings in property, unless the gain is nonrecurring.

If you voluntarily reduce your income, or quit your job, the judge can refuse to recognize the reduction or loss of income. This is *imputed income*. The only exception is where you are required to take such an action to stay home and care for your child, or show other "good cause" and can prove the change was not done to avoid paying child support (or alimony). If this question comes up, the judge will decide whether you need to stay home, so be ready to explain your reasons.

Net income. Your *net income* is determined by subtracting certain deductions from your gross income. The following deductions are allowed:

- federal, state, and local income taxes. (The amount of each deduction will be determined by the filing status and number of dependents allowable on your tax return.)
- social security (FICA), or self-employment taxes.
- mandatory union dues (where you must pay dues to keep your job).
- mandatory retirement payments (where you must contribute to keep your job).
- health insurance payments, for you and your minor child.
- court-ordered support for other children (but only if you are actually paying it).
- if you have your own business or have to pay business expenses to work at your job, the judge can allow deductions for paying these costs.

Your gross income minus these deductions will be your net income. The same process should be applied to your spouse's income to arrive at his or her net income. These deductions and net incomes will also be listed in the Financial Affidavit (Form 12) that each of you will prepare and file.

Calculating Child Support

Once you determine the net income of the party to pay child support (the party without physical custody), Section 5/505 of the Illinois Statutes (appendix A) sets out the method for calculating child support.

To assist with your calculations, use the Child Support Calculation Method (Form 3), using gross income, subtracting deductions as allowed by law, and multiplying the actual net income by the percentage which is based on the number of minor children living with the custodial parent. For example, if the net income is $500.00 per week and there are three children to support, multiply $500.00 by .32 (for 32%). The custodial parent should then receive $160.00 per week.

The figure you obtain will be a minimum amount of child support required to be paid under Illinois law. The judge can go lower or higher than the minimum guideline, but that judge will have to give a specific reason as to why the minimum is not used.

The actual calculated child support is generally paid on the basis of the payor's actual pay period (i.e., weekly, bi-weekly, or monthly), and is required to be paid through the Office of the Circuit Clerk unless otherwise agreed between the parties. The circuit clerk is the record keeper for child support payments and it is beneficial to both parties to have payments made through that office so as to avoid confusion or problems in the future.

Maintenance (Alimony)

Alimony is called *maintenance* in Illinois, and may be granted to either the husband or wife (although there are few cases where a wife will be ordered to pay alimony). The more familiar term *alimony* will be used in this book. (See Section 5/504 in appendix A for more explanation of the factors involved in determining alimony.) There are two types of alimony:

- *rehabilitative*. This is for a limited period of time, and is to enable one of the spouses to get the education or training necessary to find a job. This is usually awarded where one of the parties has not been working during the marriage.
- *permanent*. This continues for a long period of time, possibly until the death of the party receiving the alimony. This is typically awarded where one of the parties is unable to work due to age, or a physical or mental illness, or long-standing unemployment and lack of skills, particularly with a long marriage.

The factors to be considered in determining the type and amount of alimony also give clues as to when alimony might be awarded. Misconduct by one of the parties (for example, physical abuse or adultery) is not considered by the judge.

The law requires the judge to consider the following factors:

1. the income and property of each party, including marital and non-marital property assigned to the party seeking maintenance.
2. the needs of each party.
3. the present and future earning capacity of each party.
4. any impairment of the present and future earning capacity of the party seeking maintenance due to that party devoting time to domestic duties or having foregone or delayed education, training, employment, or career opportunities during the marriage.

5. the time necessary to enable the party seeking maintenance to acquire appropriate education, training, and employment, and whether that party is able to support himself or herself through appropriate employment or is the custodian of a child making it appropriate that the custodian not seek employment.
6. the standard of living established during the marriage.
7. the duration of the marriage.
8. the age and physical and emotional condition of both parties.
9. the tax consequences of property division upon the respective economic circumstances of the parties.
10. contributions and services by the party seeking maintenance to the education, training, career or career potential, or license of the other spouse.
11. any valid agreement of the parties.
12. any other factor that the court expressly finds to be just and equitable.

As an alternative to alimony, you may want to try to negotiate to receive a greater percentage of the property instead. This may be less of a hassle in the long run, but it may change the tax consequences of your divorce. (See the section in chapter 11 regarding taxes.)

Which Procedure to Use

Technically, there are two divorce procedures (simplified and regular); however, we will refer to three. These three are:

1. Simplified divorce procedure
2. Uncontested divorce procedure
3. Contested divorce procedure

The simplified procedure uses a different set of forms from the uncontested and the contested. The uncontested and contested use the same forms, but the contested will require some additional steps so it is treated as a separate procedure.

Chapter 6 of this book describes the simplified procedure, chapter 7 describes the uncontested procedure, and chapter 8 describes the contested divorce. You should read this entire book once before you begin filling out any court forms.

> ***Residency requirement.*** You or your spouse must have lived in Illinois for at least ninety days before filing your petition.

SIMPLIFIED DIVORCE PROCEDURE

To be eligible for the simplified divorce procedure you will have to be able to answer "yes" to the following questions:

1. Are you and your spouse without any minor children?
2. Are you (or your spouse) not pregnant?
3. Have you and your spouse agreed on how to divide your property?
4. Will both you and your spouse attend a court hearing?
5. Have you been married for five years or less?
6. Are you and your spouse without real estate?
7. Is the total value of all your marital property, after deducting loans on the property, less than $5,000?
8. Is the total income of both of you less than $25,000 a year?
9. Have you and your spouse been separated at least six months?

If you can answer "yes" to all nine of these questions you may use the simplified procedure. If you're not sure how to answer the first question, read the beginning of chapter 6 for more explanation.

Uncontested Divorce Procedure

If you can't qualify for the simplified procedure, you will have to use the uncontested procedure or contested procedure. The uncontested procedure is mainly designed for those who are in agreement (or can reach an agreement) about how to divide the property, but can't use the simplified procedure because there are children or too much property or income involved. This is also referred to as a *consent* divorce. It is similar to the simplified procedure, although different forms are used. The uncontested procedure may also be used when your spouse does not respond to your petition, or cannot be located.

Contested Divorce Procedure

This procedure will be necessary where you and your spouse are arguing over some matter, and can't resolve it. This may be a disagreement over custody of the children, the payment of child support or alimony, the division of your property, or any combination of these items. The section of this book dealing with the contested procedure builds on the uncontested procedure section. So, first you will need to read chapter 7 to get a basic understanding of the forms and procedures, then read chapter 8 for additional instructions on handling the contested situation. Be sure to read through both chapters before you start filling out any forms. If your case becomes contested, it is also time to seriously consider getting a lawyer. If you don't think you can afford a lawyer, you may be able to require your spouse to pay for your lawyer. Find a lawyer who will give you a free initial consultation. He or she will explain your options regarding the lawyer's fees. See chapter 3 for more information about lawyers.

GENERAL PROCEDURES 5

AN INTRODUCTION TO LEGAL FORMS

The forms included in this book are not official forms that have been approved state-wide in Illinois. No approval like this has ever been done, and the forms from court clerks may vary with each county. You would do well to visit the clerk's office to pick up any approved pre-printed forms for your county. The forms in this book are legally correct, however, one occasionally encounters a troublesome clerk or judge who is very particular about how he or she wants the forms. If you encounter any problem with the forms in this book being accepted by the clerk of judge, you can try one or more of the following:

- Ask the clerk or judge what is wrong with your form, then try to change it to suit the clerk or judge.
- Ask the clerk or judge if there is a local form available. If there is, find out where you can get it, and use it. The instructions in this book will still help you to fill them out.
- Consult a lawyer.

Do not tear the forms out of this book to file with the court. It is best to make photocopies of the forms, and keep the originals blank to use in case you make mistakes.

Although the instructions in this book will tell you to "type in" certain information, it is not absolutely necessary to use a typewriter. If typing is not possible, you can print the information required in the forms. Just be sure your handwriting can be easily read, or the clerk may not accept your papers for filing.

Each form is referred to by both the title of the form and a form number. Be sure to check the form number because some of the forms have similar titles. The form number is found in the top outside corner of the first page of each form. Also, a list of the forms, by both number and name, is found at the beginning of appendix B.

You will notice that most of the forms in appendix B of this book have the same heading. The forms without this heading are not filed with the court, but are for your use only. The top portion of these court forms will all be completed in the same manner. The heading at the very top of the form tells which court your case is filed in. You will need to type in the number of the "judicial circuit" and the county where the court is located. You can either look in the phone book, or call the court clerk's office to find out your court's circuit number.

Next, you need to type your full name, and your spouse's, on the lines at the left side of the form, below the words "In re the marriage of," above the appropriate line depending upon whether you are the petitioner (the filer of the divorce) or the respondent. Do not use nicknames or shortened versions of names. You should use the names as they appear on your marriage license, if possible. You won't be able to type in a case number until after you file your petition with the clerk. The clerk will assign a case number and will write it on your petition and any other papers you file with it. You must type in the case number on all papers you file later.

When completed, the top portion of your forms should look something like the example at the top of the next page:

IN THE CIRCUIT COURT OF THE ___THIRTEENTH___ JUDICIAL CIRCUIT, IN AND FOR ___LA SALLE___ COUNTY, ILLINOIS

IN RE: The Marriage of CASE NO:_______________

RHETT BUTLER___________________,
Petitioner,

and

SCARLETT O'HARA BUTLER________,
Respondent.

Filing with the Court Clerk

Once you have decided which forms you need, and have them all prepared, it is time to file your case with the court clerk. First, make at least three copies of each form (the original for the clerk, one copy for yourself, one for your spouse, and one extra just in case the clerk asks for two copies or you decide to hire an attorney later).

Filing is actually about as simple as making a bank deposit, although the following information will help things go smoothly. Call the court clerk's office. You can find the phone number under the county government section of your phone directory. Ask the clerk the following questions (along with any other questions that come to mind, such as where the clerk's office is located and their hours):

- How much is the filing fee for a dissolution of marriage?
- Does the court have any special forms that need to be filed with the petition? (If there are special forms that do not appear in this book, then you will need to go down to the clerk's office and pick them up. There may be a fee, so ask.)

☛ How many copies of the petition and other forms do you need to file with the clerk?

Next, take your petition, and any other forms you determine you need, to the clerk's office. The clerk handles many different types of cases, so be sure to look for signs telling you which office or window to go to. You should be looking for signs that say such things as "Family Court," "Family Division," "Filing," etc. If it's too confusing, ask someone where to file a petition for dissolution of marriage.

Once you've found the right place, simply hand the papers to the clerk and say: "I'd like to file this." The clerk will examine the papers, then do one of two things: either accept it for filing (and either collect the filing fee or direct you to where to pay it), or tell you that something is not correct. If you're told something is wrong, ask the clerk to explain to you what is wrong and how to correct the problem. Although clerks are not permitted to give legal advice, the types of problems they spot are usually very minor things that they can tell you how to correct. Often it is possible to figure out how to correct it from the way they explain what is wrong.

Notifying Your Spouse

If you are using the simplified divorce procedure you do not need to worry about the information in this section (your spouse will have to sign the petition, so it will be obvious that he or she knows about the divorce). Also, you don't need to worry about this section if you and your spouse are in agreement about everything, but don't qualify for the simplified procedure. Your spouse can simply file a Response to Petition for Dissolution of Marriage (Form 13), a Financial Affidavit (Form 12), or you can both sign and file a settlement agreement (Form 10 or Form 19). However, in all other cases, you are required to notify your spouse that you have filed for divorce.This gives your spouse a chance to respond to your Petition for Dissolution of Marriage. If you are unable to find your spouse, you will also need to read chapter 10.

Notice of Filing the Petition for Dissolution of Marriage

The usual way to notify your spouse that you filed for a divorce is called *personal service*, which is where the sheriff, or someone else designated by the judge, personally delivers the papers to your spouse. The sheriff deputy will need copies of your Petition for Dissolution of Marriage, any affidavits you filed, and a summons. A *summons* is a form you will obtain from the court clerk, which informs your spouse of his or her rights, and obligation to answer the petition.

To arrange for service, call the county sheriff's office in the county where your spouse lives, and ask how much it will cost to have him or her served with divorce papers. It will probably cost from $15.00 to $30.00. Deliver, or mail, one copy of your Petition for Dissolution of Marriage (together with the affidavits you filed), two copies of a Summons, and a check or money order for the service fee, to the sheriff's office.

To complete the summons (refer to the sample summons on page 69) you need to:

1. Go to the clerk's office, and have the clerk sign a summons (an approved form that the clerk will provide you).
2. Complete the top portion according to the instructions in the first section of this chapter.
3. Type in the name of the proper courthouse on the line in the first paragraph.
4. Type in the name of the county on the line after the word "Witness."
5. Type your name, address, and phone number on the line after the words "Petitioner or Attorney," and type in your address and phone on the lines indicated.

A sample summons is shown at the end of this chapter. A sheriff's deputy will personally deliver the papers to your spouse. Of course, you must give the sheriff accurate information about where your spouse can be found. If there are several addresses where your spouse might be found (such as home, a relative's, and work), enclose a letter to the sheriff with all of the addresses and any other information which may help the sheriff find your spouse (such as the hours your spouse works). The deputy will fill out a form to verify that the papers were delivered (including the date and time they were delivered), and will file a copy of that form with the court clerk.

Other Notices

Once your spouse has been served with the Petition for Dissolution of Marriage, you may simply mail him or her copies of any papers you file later. All you need to do is sign a statement (called a *Proof of Service*) that you mailed copies to your spouse. Some of the forms in this book will have a certificate of service for you to complete. If any form you file does not contain one, you will need to complete the Proof of Service (Form 6). To complete Form 6:

1. Complete the top portion according to the instructions in the first section of this chapter.
2. Type in the name or title of the papers being sent on the first line of the first paragraph (e.g., "Petition," "Motion," etc.).
3. Type in the name of the person to whom the documents will be sent (your spouse or your spouse's attorney, the city they were sent from, and the date they were sent.
4. Sign your name (before a notary public) on the line marked "Signature." This form is to be filed with the court clerk as your proof that you sent a copy. ***Caution:*** This form must be notarized.

Once you get a hearing date set with the judge, you'll need to notify your spouse of when the hearing will be. This is done by preparing a Notice (Form 5). Just fill in the top of the form according to the instructions in the first section of this chapter, and fill in all of the blanks on the form for the day of the week, date, month, year, time, judge's name, location of the hearing, your signature, and your name, address, and phone number. Then make three copies of the Notice, and mail one copy to your spouse. File the original with the court clerk, and keep two copies for yourself. If child support or alimony is requested by you, you will also need to file a completed Financial Affidavit (Form 12) in most counties. You should send your spouse a copy of it.

Setting a Court Hearing

You will need to set a hearing date for the final hearing, or for any preliminary matters which require a hearing (these will be discussed later in this book). The court clerk will give you a date for the judge assigned to your case. Be sure you get the location also, including the street address of the courthouse, and the room number, floor, or other location within the building. (If you don't know which judge, call the court clerk, give the clerk your case number, and ask for the name and phone number of the judge assigned to your case.) You can then either call or go see that judge's clerk and tell him or her you'd like to set a final hearing date for a dissolution of marriage (or for whatever preliminary motion needs a hearing). Usually the judge's phone number can be found in the government section of your phone book.

The clerk may ask you how long the hearing will take. If you are using the simplified divorce procedure, tell the clerk, and he or she will probably know how much time to allow (usually about ten minutes). If you are unable to use the simplified procedure, but you and your spouse have agreed on everything (an uncontested divorce), tell the clerk it is an uncontested divorce and ask for ten minutes (unless he or she advises you differently). If you have a contested divorce, it could take anywhere from thirty minutes to several days, depending upon such things as what matters you disagree about and how many witnesses will testify. One general rule of thumb is that the more time you need for a hearing, the longer it will take to get the hearing. Also, it is better to over-estimate the time required, rather than not schedule enough time and have to continue the hearing for several weeks. The judge may not go over the time scheduled!

Some judges may insist that you file a Notice (Form 5), specifying the type of hearing. If your judge requires this, use the Notice (Form 5) and Proof of Service (Form 6). Your next step will be to notify your spouse of the hearing (see the previous section of this chapter). If the judge requires a motion to set a trial or hearing, use the Motion to Set Hearing (Form 4) (fill out the top portion and sign it).

Courtroom Manners

There are certain rules of procedure that are used in a court. These are really the rules of good conduct, or good manners, and are designed to keep things orderly. Many of the rules are written down, although some are unwritten customs that have just developed over many years. They aren't difficult, and most of them do make sense. Following these suggestions will make the judge respect you for your maturity and professional manner, and possibly even make him forget for a moment that you are not a lawyer. It will also increase the likelihood that you will get the things you request.

Respect

Show respect for the judge. This basically means, don't do anything to make the judge angry at you, such as arguing with him. Be polite, and call the judge "Your Honor" when you speak to him, such as "Yes, Your Honor," or "Your Honor, I brought proof of my income." Although many, many lawyers address judges as "Judge," this is not proper. Many of the following rules also relate to showing respect for the court. This also means wearing appropriate clothing, such as a coat and tie for men and a dress for women. This especially means no T-shirts, blue jeans, shorts, or "revealing" clothing.

Courtesy

Whenever the judge talks, you listen. Even if the judge interrupts you, stop talking immediately and listen.

One at a Time

Only one person can talk at a time. Each person is allotted his or her own time to talk in court. The judge can only listen to one person at a time, so don't interrupt your spouse when it's his or her turn. And as difficult as it may be, stop talking if your spouse interrupts you. (Let the judge tell your spouse to keep quiet and let you have your say.)

Talk to the Judge, Not to Your Spouse

Many people get in front of a judge and begin arguing with each other. They actually turn away from the judge, face each other, and begin arguing as if they are in the room alone. This generally has several negative results: The judge can't understand what either one is saying since they both start talking at once, they both look like fools for losing control, and the judge gets angry with both of them. So whenever you speak in a courtroom, look only at the judge. Try to pretend that your spouse isn't there. Remember, you are there to convince the judge that you should have certain things. You don't need to convince your spouse.

Wait Your Turn

Talk only when it's your turn. The usual procedure is for you to present your case first. When you are done saying all you came to say, your spouse will have a chance to say whatever he or she came to say. Let your spouse have his or her say. When your spouse is finished you will get another chance to respond to what has been said.

Stick to the Subject

Many people can't resist the temptation to get off the track and start telling the judge all the problems with their marriage over the past twenty years. This just wastes time, and aggravates the judge. So stick to the subject, and answer the judge's questions simply and to the point.

Keep Calm

Judges like things to go smoothly in their courtrooms. They don't like shouting, name calling, crying, or other displays of emotion. Generally, judges don't like family law cases because they get too emotionally charged. So give your judge a pleasant surprise by keeping calm and focusing on the issues.

Show Respect for Your Spouse

Even if you don't respect your spouse, act like you do. All you have to do is refer to your spouse as "Mr. Smith" or "Ms. Smith" (using his or her correct name, of course).

Negotiating

It is beyond the scope and ability of this book to fully present a course in negotiation techniques. However, a few basic rules may be of some help.

Ask for More than You Want

Asking for more than you want always gives you some room to compromise by giving up a few things, and end up with close to what you really want. With property division, this means you will review your Property Inventory (Form 1), and decide which items you really want, would like to have, and don't care much about. Also try to figure out which items your spouse really wants, would like to have, and doesn't care much about. At the beginning you will say that you want certain things. Your list will include:

1. Everything you really want.
2. Almost everything you'd like to have.
3. Some of the things you don't care about.
4. Some of the things you think your spouse really wants or would like to have.

Once you find out what is on your spouse's list, you begin trading items. Generally you try to give your spouse things that he really wants and that you don't care about, in return for your spouse giving you the items you really care about and would like to have.

Generally, child custody tends to be something which cannot be negotiated. It is more often used as a threat by one of the parties in order to get something else, such as more of the property, or lower child support. If the real issue is one of these other matters, don't be concerned by a threat of a custody fight. In these cases the other party probably doesn't really want custody, and won't fight for it. If the real issue is custody, you won't be able to negotiate for it and will end up letting the judge decide anyway.

If you will be receiving child support you should first work out what you think the judge will order based upon the child support guidelines discussed in chapter 4. Then you should ask for more, and negotiate down to the guidelines. If your spouse won't settle for something very close to the guidelines, give up trying to work it out and let the judge decide. The judge will not approve an agreement that is not very close or greater to the minimum percentages (for percentages, see Form 3).

Let Your Spouse Start the Bidding

The first person to mention a dollar figure loses. Whether it's a child support figure or the value of a piece of property, try to get your spouse to name the amount he or she thinks it should be first. If your spouse starts with a figure almost what you had in mind, it will be much easier to get to your figure. If your spouse begins with a figure far from yours, you know how far in the other direction to begin your bid.

Give Your Spouse Time to Think and Worry

Your spouse is probably just as afraid as you about the possibility of losing to the judge's decision, and would like to settle. Don't be afraid to state your "final offer," then walk away. Give your spouse a day or two to think it over. Maybe he or she will call back and make a better offer. If not, you can always "reconsider" and make a different offer in a few days, but don't be too willing to do this or your spouse may think you will give in even more.

Know Your Bottom Line

Before you begin negotiating you should try to set a point which you will not go beyond. If you have decided that there are four items of property that you absolutely must have, and your spouse is only willing to agree to let you have three, it's time to end the bargaining session and go home.

Remember what you've learned:

1. The judge will roughly divide your property equally.

2. The judge will probably come very close to the child support minimum guidelines.

This awareness should give you an approximate idea of how things will turn out if the judge is asked to decide these issues, which should help you to set your bottom line.

Sample Summons

IN THE CIRCUIT COURT OF THE THIRTEENTH JUDICIAL CIRCUIT
LA SALLE COUNTY

Jane Doe
vs. Petitioner
John Doe
Respondent

No. 98-D-1509

SUMMONS
ILLINOIS MARRIAGE AND DISSOLUTION OF MARRIAGE ACT

To each Defendant:

You are summoned and required to file an answer to the complaint in this case, a copy of which is hereto attached, or otherwise file your appearance in the office of the Clerk of this Court, LaSalle Co. Courthouse, Ottawa, Illinois, within 30 days after service of this summons, not counting the day of service. IF YOU FAIL TO DO SO, A JUDGMENT BY DEFAULT MAY BE TAKEN AGAINST YOU FOR THE RELIEF ASKED IN THE COMPLAINT.

YOU ARE FURTHER NOTIFIED THAT A DISSOLUTION ACTION STAY IS IN FULL FORCE AND EFFECT UPON SERVICE OF THIS SUMMONS. THE CONDITIONS OF THE STAY ARE SET FORTH ON THE REVERSE SIDE OF DEFENDANTS COPY OF THE SUMMONS, AND ARE APPLICABLE TO THE PARTIES AS SET FORTH IN THE STATUTE. (750 ILCS 5/501.1) Chap 40, Par. 501.1, I.R.S.

To the Officer:

This summons must be returned by the Officer or other person to whom it was given for service, with endorsement of service and fees, if any immediately after service. If service cannot be made, this summons shall be returned so endorsed. This summons may not be served later than 30 days after its date.

WITNESS: LA SALLE County Circuit Clerk,
and the seal thereof, at Ottawa, Illinois.
Dated ______, ______

Ottawa Circuit Clerk

Note: The filing of an appearance or answer with the Circuit Court Clerk requires a statutory filing fee, payable at the time of filing.

Petitioner or Attorney Jane Doe
Address 123 Joliet Ave.
City Ottawa, IL
Phone (815) 555-9999

Date of Service ______, ______
To be inserted by the officer on copy left with defendant or other person

SHERIFF'S FEES

Service and return $______ Miles ______ = $______ Total $______

I certify that I served this summons on the defendant by leaving a copy and a copy of the complaint with (a)__ the individual defendant personally (b)__ at the usual place of abode of the defendant with a person of his family, of age 13 years or upwards, informing that person of the contents and also by sending a copy of this summons in a sealed envelope with postage fully prepaid, addressed to the individual defendant at his usual place of abode.

Signature ______, Sheriff of ______ County
Name of Defendant ______ Name of Person Summons given to ______
Sex ______ Race ______ Approx. Age ______ Place of Service ______
Date of Service ______ Time ______ am/pm Date of Mailing ______

Simplified Divorce Procedure 6

Can You Use the Simplified Procedure?

In certain circumstances you may take advantage of Illinois' Simplified Dissolution of Marriage procedure. In order to use this procedure you must meet the following basic requirements:

1. You or your spouse have resided in Illinois for at least the past ninety days.
2. You and your spouse do not have any minor or dependent children. (A minor child is one who is under the age of eighteen. A dependent child may be over the age of eighteen, but is still dependent upon you for support due to mental or physical illness, disease or disability. You may still use the procedure if you have children from a prior marriage, as long as your current spouse has not adopted them.)
3. The wife is not pregnant.
4. You and your spouse have agreed as to how your property will be divided.
5. You and your spouse will both attend the court hearing.
6. You have been married five years or less.

7. You and your spouse do not own any real estate.
8. You and your spouse have less than $5,000 in property.
9. You and your spouse have a combined income of less than $25,000 a year.
10. You and your spouse must have been separated at least six months and agree that "irreconcilable differences" have caused a breakdown of the marriage.

If you don't meet all ten of these conditions, you may not use the simplified procedure. However, you may still want to read this section, as it may help you understand the standard procedure better. If the only requirement you don't meet is that you can't agree on the division of your property, you may want to reconsider your position on the property. Read this chapter, and have your spouse read it. Then compare the simplified procedure to the standard procedures in chapter 7 and chapter 8 of this book. Once you see how much easier the simplified procedure is, you may want to try harder to resolve your differences over the property. The simplified procedure can take as little time as it takes to complete the forms and arrange for the judge to hear the agreement in court. Basically, the procedure is as follows:

1. You and your spouse complete the necessary forms.
2. You file the appropriate forms with the court clerk.
3. You and your spouse appear for a brief hearing with the judge.

The following is a discussion of the possible forms used in the simplified procedure, and of the procedure itself. You will definitely need to use five of these forms, and may need one or both of the others depending upon your situation. ***Caution:*** You should also be aware that, with the simplified procedure, neither party may receive alimony and there is no appeal.

JOINT PETITION FOR SIMPLIFIED DISSOLUTION OF MARRIAGE

FORM 7

The Joint Petition for Simplified Dissolution of Marriage (Form 7) is the paper used to open your case and ask for a divorce. To complete the Joint Petition for Simplified Dissolution of Marriage (Form 7):

1. Complete the top portion according to the instructions in chapter 5.
2. Type in your name on the first line in the first, unnumbered paragraph, and your spouse's name on the second line.
3. In paragraph 1, type in your age, occupation, and residence address, and check the box to indicate that you have lived in Illinois at least ninety days before filing the petition. You should file your divorce papers in the county where you live.
4. In paragraph 2, fill in the same information for your spouse.
5. In paragraph 3, fill in the date of your marriage, and the county and state where you were married.
6. In paragraph 4, type in the wife's name.
7. In paragraph 5, fill in the date of your separation.
8. In paragraph 9, fill in your annual income and your spouse's annual income.
9. If the wife wants her former name restored, fill in paragraph 11, and repeat this information in paragraph C.
10. Go with your spouse to a notary public, and sign on the appropriate signature lines before the notary. This form will now be ready for filing with the court clerk.

FINANCIAL AFFIDAVIT

FORM 12

You should only complete the Financial Affidavit (Form 12) if the clerk or judge tells you to complete it. Otherwise, there is really no reason to put your financial affairs in a court file that anyone can see (divorce court files are public records). Of course, if the clerk or judge requires financial affidavits, you will have to file them. If financial affidavits are needed, you and your spouse must each file one. See chapter 7 for instructions on how to complete the Financial Affidavit form, if you find one is needed.

AGREEMENT AS TO ASSETS AND DEBTS

FORM 10

The Agreement as to Assets and Debts (Form 10) spells out how your property and debts will be divided. To complete the Agreement as to Assets and Debts (Form 10) you need to:

1. Complete the top portion according to the instructions in chapter 5.
2. Type your name and your spouse's name in the two spaces in the first paragraph. *Plaintiff* is the person filing or starting the divorce with the simplified procedure, it does matter which of you is the plaintiff.
3. List the items of property and who is to receive it. Be as specific in describing the items as you were in Form 1 which you completed back in chapter 4. You don't need to include every little item in the house, but you should include all major items. If you need more space to list all the property, attach another sheet of paper.
4. List all debts, their current balances, account number if applicable, and who will pay each debt.

5. On the last page of the form, you and your spouse need to sign before the court clerk or a notary public. This can be done when you file your petition.

Joint Affidavit Regarding Separation of the Parties

FORM 8

The joint simplified procedure in Illinois requires that no-fault grounds be used as the reason for the joint simplified divorce. You cannot give reasons like mental cruelty, adultery, or any other legal ground. You must have been separated at least six months to get a no-fault divorce and use the joint simplified procedure.

The Joint Affidavit Regarding Separation of the Parties (Form 8) must be completed and signed by you and your spouse before a notary to verify to the judge that you and your spouse have been separated at least six months; that you are *waiving*, or giving up, your right to insist on a maximum separation time of two years; and that you both want to proceed with the divorce at one court hearing, since Illinois otherwise requires a hearing on the grounds and a separate hearing on custody and property matters (this system is called a *bifurcated hearing*).

The Joint Affidavit Regarding Separation of the Parties (Form 8) is filed with the clerk at the same time as the Joint Petition for Simplified Dissolution of Marriage (Form 7).

Judgment for Dissolution of Marriage

FORM 9

The Judgment for Dissolution of Marriage (Form 9) is the paper the judge will sign at the final hearing to formally grant a divorce. To complete the Judgment for Dissolution of Marriage (Form 9) you will need to:

1. Complete the top portion of the form according to the instructions in chapter 5.
2. Type in the husband's and wife's names on the appropriate lines.
3. Fill in paragraph 11 and relief letter if the wife is resuming her maiden name.
4. Sign approval lines.

The judge will fill in the date and sign the form at the final hearing.

Certificate of Dissolution of Marriage

This form is required by the courts to register the divorce locally and with the division of vital records in the State Public Health Department. The form is supplied by the clerk of the court and is completed and filed at the time the final judgement is signed.

7 Uncontested Divorce Procedure

This chapter will provide a general overview of the standard divorce procedure. If you and your spouse are in agreement, but don't qualify for the simplified procedure, you will need to follow the procedures in this chapter.

Most lawyers have had the following experience: A new client comes in, saying she wants to file for divorce. She has discussed it with her husband, and it will be a "simple, uncontested" divorce. Once the papers are filed the husband and wife begin arguing over a few items of property. The lawyer then spends a lot of time negotiating with the husband. After much arguing, an agreement is finally reached. The case will proceed in the court as "uncontested," but only after a lot of "contesting" out of court.

For purposes of this book, a *contested* case is one where you and your spouse will be doing your arguing in court, and leaving the decision up to the judge. An *uncontested* case is one where you will do your arguing and deciding before court, and the judge will only be approving your decision.

You probably won't know if you are going to have a contested case until you try the uncontested route and fail. Therefore, the following sections are presented mostly to assist you in attempting the uncontested case. Chapter 8 specifically discusses the contested case.

There are actually two ways that a case can be considered uncontested. One is where you and your spouse reach an agreement on every issue in the divorce, but can't use the simplified procedure because you have a minor child, real estate or income over $25,000, or have not been separated for six months. To be in this situation, you must be in agreement on the following points:

1. how your property is to be divided.
2. how your debts are to be divided.
3. who will have custody of the children.
4. how much child support is to be paid by the person without custody.
5. whether alimony is to be paid, and if so, how much and for how long a period of time.

The other type of uncontested case is where your spouse simply doesn't respond to the petition. If you have your spouse served by the sheriff (as described in chapter 5), and he or she does not respond, you will need to file certain forms. This is called a *default divorce*.

To begin your divorce case, you must file a Petition for Dissolution of Marriage (Form 11). Other forms that you determine to be necessary will also be filed (such as a Financial Affidavit, etc.), either with your Petition for Dissolution of Marriage or at any time before the final hearing, depending upon your situation. The following forms will be prepared in advance, but will not be filed until the final hearing:

1. Judgment of Dissolution of Marriage (Form 20).
2. Certificate of Dissolution (Form supplied by clerk).
3. if child support is to be paid, an Order for Withholding (Form 21).

Once all of the necessary forms have been filed, you will need to call the judge's secretary to arrange for a hearing date for the final judgment (see chapter 5 regarding setting a hearing). You should tell the secretary that you need to schedule a "final hearing for an uncontested divorce." Such a hearing should not usually take more than ten minutes. See chapter 9 for information on how to handle the final hearing. The following sections give instructions for when you need each form, and how to complete it.

Petition for Dissolution of Marriage

FORM 11

The Petition for Dissolution of Marriage (Form 11) must be completed in all cases, except for the simplified procedure. The Petition for Dissolution of Marriage (Form 11) is simply the paper you file with the court to begin your case and to ask the judge to give you a divorce. The Petition for Dissolution of Marriage should be accompanied by your Financial Affidavit (Form 12), which gives the judge part of the financial information he may need. The Petition for Dissolution of Marriage may also be accompanied by other affidavits, depending upon your situation. Together, these papers give the judge an idea of your situation, and of what you want him to do.

To complete your Petition for Dissolution of Marriage (Form 11), you need to do the following:

1. Complete the top portion of the form, according to the instructions in chapter 5.
2. In the first, unnumbered paragraph, type your name in the blank space.
3. In paragraph 1, type in your age, your current residence address, and the date you first began residing in Illinois. Also type in the name and address of your employer (if you are not employed, type in "none").
4. In paragraph 2, type in your spouse's age, current residence address, and the date your spouse first began residing in Illinois.

Also type in the name and address of your spouse's employer (if your spouse is not employed, type in "none").

5. In paragraph 3, type in the date you were married, the city, county, and state where you were married.

6. If you have been separated for more than six months and are using paragraph 6(b) as your grounds for divorce, you will need to complete paragraph 5, by typing in the date you and your spouse separated. Otherwise, strike out paragraph 5.

7. In paragraph 6, choose which *ground* you are claiming for divorce. Paragraph (a) is mental cruelty. Paragraph (b) is "no-fault," but this requires at least six months of separation and the agreement of your spouse to waive the two-year waiting period. Complete and attach the Stipulation (Form 15), by filling in the blanks, and both you and your spouse signing.

8. In paragraph 7, type in the number of children born of your marriage, and complete and fill in all blanks with proper names, addresses, ages, and dates, including the names of children and their dates of birth. If you don't have children, type in the words "no children." Check the appropriate line to indicate whether the wife is pregnant. If she is pregnant, the judge can still grant a divorce, but will reserve the questions of birth expenses, child support, custody, and visitation until after the birth.

9. In paragraph 8, fill in the name of each creditor and the amount owed, for all debts accumulated during the marriage.

10. In paragraph 9, list all property accumulated during the marriage. You do not need to get into pots and pans but can generally refer to those items, as well as furniture, as "household furnishings." Larger items such as real estate, vehicles, and any item in excess of $1,000.00 in value should be specifically described.

11. In paragraph 11, you may type in miscellaneous requests, such as repayment of your attorney fees by your spouse, or alimony (maintenance) payments.
12. If you are not requesting custody of children, or have no children, you can strike out the appropriate paragraphs to reflect your situation.
13. On the last page, in paragraph 3, type in the county where you will file.
14. Once you have completed the form, take it to a notary public, and sign on the line marked "Petitioner." The notary will complete the rest of the form. Take it to the clerk for filing.

Your Petition for Dissolution of Marriage is now ready for filing. If you need to have your spouse served by the sheriff, be sure to prepare the Summons to go along with your Petition for Dissolution of Marriage (see the section on the Summons in chapter 5).

Financial Affidavit

Form 12

The Financial Affidavit (Form 12) should be completed if there are any matters that you and your spouse don't agree upon, or if directed by the clerk or judge. If it is to be completed, you and your spouse must each file one. The Financial Affidavit is based on monthly income and expenses. If you are paid weekly, or every two weeks, you will need to convert your income to a monthly figure. The same conversion will be required for any of your expenses that are not paid monthly. To convert weekly amounts to monthly amounts, just take the weekly figure and multiply it by 4.3. (There are roughly 4.3 weeks to a month.) To convert from every two weeks, divide by 2 and then multiply by 4.3.

Fill in all of the blank spaces on the Financial Affidavit form, then take it to a notary public before you sign it. You will sign it before the notary, then staple it to your Petition for Dissolution of Marriage (after you have made two copies). Most of the blanks in the Financial Affidavit clearly indicate what information is to be filled in; however, the following may answer some questions:

1. Complete the top portion of the form according to the instructions in chapter 5.
2. Type in your name in the blank in the first paragraph.
3. Item 4 refers to "Monthly Expenses." Simply refer to each item listed and estimate as best you can the amount you spend on that item in a month. If a particular item is an annual expense, such as auto insurance, convert it to a monthly amount.
4. To complete Item 4 on "Debts," refer to the list on Form 2 and to chapter 5.
5. To complete Item 7 on "Assets," refer to the list on Form 1, and to chapter 5.
6. Take the form to a notary and sign it before the notary on the line designated "Affiant." The notary will complete the part of the form directly below your signature, or take it to the circuit clerk to witness your signature.

Marital Settlement Agreement for Dissolution of Marriage

Form 19

The Marital Settlement Agreement for Dissolution of Marriage (Form 19) is broad in scope and should be carefully completed. It includes provisions for agreements on child support and custody, alimony, and attorneys fees. Whether you and your spouse agreed on everything from the start, or whether you've gone through extensive negotiations to reach an agreement, you need to put your agreement in writing. Even if you don't agree on everything, you should put what you do agree on into a written settlement agreement. To complete the Marital

Settlement Agreement for Dissolution of Marriage (Form 19) you need to:

1. Complete the top portion according to the instructions in chapter 5.

2. Type in your name and your spouse's name in the blanks in the first paragraph; and type in the date you were married.

3. In each section check the box for the provision that applies to your situation. Read through each one and look for places where you need to mark a box or type in information to fit your situation.

4. You will type in the names of your children in the "Child Custody" section. Physical custody refers to whom each child will live with as the child's permanent residence. Any special arrangements you wish to include in this section can be typed in by the last box in this section.

5. The section on "Child Support" will require you to type in an amount and a period, such as "$583.20" per "month." You will also need to check the box for either "Husband" or "Wife" in the sections on child support and health insurance. Illinois law requires that provisions for health insurance be in every divorce judgment.

6. Refer to the instructions in chapter 7 regarding how to complete the sections on the division of property and debts (which are basically the same as in Form 9).

7. There are three possible boxes to check in the "Alimony" section of Form 19. Check the first box if no alimony is to be paid by either you or your spouse. The second box is to be checked if you and your spouse have agreed to alimony. If so, you will also need to check the appropriate box for who is to pay the alimony, and fill in the amount, when that amount is to be paid (weekly, monthly, etc.), and for how long. For rehabilitative alimony, this

time will be until a specific date. For permanent alimony, just cross out the words "for a period of." The last box is to check if there are any special agreements regarding alimony.

8. If either or both of you consulted (and were charged by) an attorney, fill in who will pay that lawyer. Otherwise leave that section blank.

9. Each of you should sign and date the form where indicated at the bottom, then file it with the court clerk. It is a good idea to sign before a notary, if possible.

Response to Petition for Dissolution of Marriage

FORM 13

Unless you use the simplified procedure, if you and your spouse can agree on everything and both of you sign and file a Marital Settlement Agreement (Form 19), your spouse still needs to complete the Response to Petition for Dissolution of Marriage (Form 13). If you and your spouse are in full agreement about the divorce, you can simplify and speed up the case by having your spouse sign Form 13 before a notary public. If Form 13 is used, you will not need to go through the procedure in chapter 5 on notifying your spouse, and you will not need to complete the Affidavit as to Military Service (Form 16), because you both have agreed to the terms of the divorce.

To complete the Response to Petition for Dissolution of Marriage (Form 13) you need to:

1. Complete the top portion according to the instructions in chapter 5.

2. Type in your spouse's name in the blank space in the first paragraph.

3. Type in your spouse's name below the "Respondent" line.

4. Have your spouse sign on the "Respondent" line before a notary public.

If you and your spouse cannot agree and the case will be contested, your spouse will need to file a Response to Petition for Dissolution of Marriage, admitting or denying the statements in your Petition for Dissolution of Marriage. This must be done by your spouse, without your help, since there is no agreement between you.

Affidavit as to Military Service

Form 16

If your spouse is not in the military service, and will not sign either a Marital Settlement Agreement (Form 19) or the Response to Petition for Dissolution of Marriage (Form 13) or file his or her own answer, you will need to complete the Affidavit as to Military Service (Form 16). To complete Form 16 you need to:

1. Complete the top portion of the form according to the instructions in chapter 5.
2. Type your name in the blank space in the first (unnumbered) paragraph.
3. Check either paragraph 1 or 2, whichever applies. You will also need to type in your spouse's name if you check paragraph 2.
4. Type in the date; your name, address, and phone number below the signature line; and complete the certificate of service section.
5. Sign before a notary public on the line above the word "Signature of Affiant."

Call the court clerk to ask when the Affidavit as to Military Service needs to be filed. Some courts require that it not be signed too far in advance, because they want the information to be reasonably current. Some courts require that the notary public's date on the Affidavit as to Military Service be within a certain number of days before filing a

Motion to Enter Default (Form 18), or before the final hearing. Some courts may not even require the affidavit to be filed.

If your spouse is not willing to file a Response to Petition for Dissolution of Marriage (Form 13), a Marital Settlement Agreement (Form 10 or Form 19), or a Financial Affidavit (Form 12), and is in the military service, do not complete the Affidavit as to Military Service, but see a lawyer. Federal laws designed to protect service personnel while overseas can create special problems in these situations.

Certificate of Military Service

FORM 17

If you don't know if your spouse is in the military service, you will need to complete the Certificate of Military Service (Form 17). To complete Form 17:

1. Complete the top portion of the form according to the instructions in chapter 5.
2. Type your spouse's name and social security number on the lines marked "Party" and "Soc. Sec. #."
3. Type in the date on the line indicated, and your name, address, and telephone number under the "Signature" line.
4. Sign the form on the line marked "Signature."

You will then need to make seven copies of this form, and mail one to each of the seven addresses listed on the form (one to each branch of the U.S. Government considered military service). Be sure to enclose a stamped envelope, addressed to yourself with each one. Each service branch will then check its records and mail you a notice as to whether your spouse is in that branch (these notices may then be filed with the court clerk). If your spouse is in one of the service branches, his or her address will be provided.

A fee may be charged by the military. Try checking on this with your closest military base, the court clerk, or the child support enforcement office. Otherwise, the branch of the military will let you know if a fee is required when it receives the form. You can then send your spouse notice of the divorce, and see if some agreement can be reached so you can use the uncontested procedure. If your spouse cannot be contacted, or will not cooperate (by either filing a Response to Petition for Dissolution of Marriage, a Financial Affidavit, or a Marital Settlement Agreement), you should contact an attorney.

MOTION TO ENTER DEFAULT

FORM 18

If your spouse does not file a Response to Petition for Dissolution of Marriage, Financial Affidavit, or join you in a Marital Settlement Agreement, within thirty days after the sheriff delivers the petition, your spouse is *in default*. You will need to notify the court clerk that your spouse has not filed a Response to Petition for Dissolution of Marriage, and ask the clerk to have the judge enter the default in your court file. To accomplish this you need to complete a Motion to Enter Default (Form 18), and deliver it to the clerk. The judge may want you to briefly testify on the failure of your spouse to respond.

To complete the Motion to Enter Default (Form 18) you need to:

1. Complete the top portion of the form according to the instructions in chapter 5.

2. Fill in the date, sign your name on the "Signature" line, and type your name, address, and phone number below the line.

The clerk will complete the bottom portion of the form, and return a copy to you. Once the default has been entered by the clerk, you are ready to have a hearing date set.

Judgment of Dissolution of Marriage

FORM 20 This form will be completed in all cases, except the simplified procedure which has its own special form. You should complete as much of the Judgment of Dissolution of Marriage as possible before the hearing. The Judgment of Dissolution of Marriage (Form 20) is designed so that you can complete it at the hearing according to what the judge decides on each issue. You can complete ahead of time any items upon which you and your spouse have agreed. You should give your spouse a copy of the Judgment of Dissolution of Marriage before the hearing, so that he or she can tell the judge that he or she is aware of what it says, and agrees with it.

To complete the Judgment of Dissolution of Marriage (Form 20) you need to:

1. Complete the top portion according to the instructions in chapter 5.
2. Type in your name and your spouse's name in the appropriate blanks in the first paragraph. You will now check the box before each of the paragraphs numbered 1 through 12 that apply to your situation, according to the following guidelines.
3. Paragraph 1: Check the box if you and your spouse signed a settlement agreement.
4. Paragraph 2: Check the box if the wife will have her former name restored, and type her restored name in the blank.
5. Paragraph 3: Type in each child's name, date of birth, and either the word "Husband" or "Wife" depending upon which one will take custody of that child.
6. Paragraph 4: Check the box for "Husband" or "Wife," whichever one will be paying child support. Type in the amount of the

support payment, how often it will be paid (week, month, etc.), and the date the first payment is due.

7. Paragraph 5: Check either "Husband" or "Wife," whichever will be responsible for health insurance for the children.

8. Paragraph 6: Complete this section on alimony the same as the child support section, and check the appropriate boxes. The first box has a blank in which to type the date the alimony payments will end, in the event temporary alimony is awarded. The second box designates permanent alimony. The law now requires the judgment to give the reasons why alimony is, or is not, awarded. It makes sense that this is only required where the judge is asked to make this decision, but the law is poorly written so that some judges may require this even where the parties have agreed on this point. The third box is for when you and your spouse have agreed on the question of alimony, so just check the appropriate box. The fourth box is for where the judge decides this question. You will need to type in, or write in, the judge's reasons.

9. Paragraphs 7, 8, 9, and 10 are to cover the division of your property and debts. These will be the same items covered in your settlement agreement (Form 9 or Form 19), in which case you can leave these paragraphs blank as they are already covered in paragraph 1 of this form. These paragraphs will be used when you do not have a settlement agreement, and the judge has decided who will get what assets and who will pay what debts.

10. Paragraph 11: Again, if you filed a settlement agreement you do not need to complete this paragraph. If there was a dispute as to what nonmarital assets and debts belong to you and your spouse, you will need to complete this paragraph after the judge has decided this question.

11. Paragraph 12: This is a space to write in any other agreements, or orders of the judge.

12. The date and signature lines are for the judge to fill in.

Be sure to check the box in front of each paragraph that applies to your situation. If a certain paragraph does not apply, simply leave it blank.

If you and your spouse have agreed to everything, you can prepare the Judgment of Dissolution of Marriage before the hearing, and give it to the judge to sign at the end of the hearing. If the judge tells you to change something major in the Judgment of Dissolution of Marriage, or if you had a contested hearing, it may not be possible to prepare it at the hearing. You will need to make a note of exactly what changes the judge requires, or what he ordered, then go home and prepare the Judgment of Dissolution of Marriage the way the judge instructed. You will then need to take the revised form back to the judge for his signature.

If you need to prepare the Judgment of Dissolution of Marriage after the hearing, you will also complete the Proof of Service (Form 6) attach it to the Judgment of Dissolution of Marriage, and deliver it to the clerk's office.

Also give the clerk two extra copies, along with a stamped envelope addressed to yourself and a stamped envelope addressed to your spouse. Ask the secretary whether you should sign and date the Proof of Service. Sometimes the secretary will handle mailing the judgment after the judge signs it, in which case he or she may sign the Proof of Service.

Certificate of Dissolution of Marriage

The Certificate of Dissolution of Marriage is a biographical sheet that the clerk will provide to you to fill out and return to the clerk. It is sent to the Division of Vital Records of the Illinois Department of Public Health.

Notice to Withhold Income for Child Support

Form 21

The Notice to Withhold Income for Child Support (Form 21) must be completed in all cases where child support or alimony is to be paid. Illinois law requires all such payments to be made by such a notice. This is an order to the employer of the person required to make the payment, requiring the employer to deduct the payment from the person's paycheck and send it to the clerk of the court. This form is to be prepared before the final hearing, and is to be presented to the judge at the hearing. *Note:* The clerk will assist you in the completion of this form if you need help.

To complete the Notice to Withhold Income for Child Support (Form 21):

1. Complete the top portion of the form, including the county of the issuing court, date, and court case number.

2. Type in the name of the person (you or your spouse) who must pay support ("employee/obligor"), and the obligor's social security number. Then type in the name of the person having custody of the child.

3. Type in the name and address of the paying person's employer and the federal employer identification number (EIN) if you know it. If not, leave the EIN line blank.

4. Fill in the names of your children and their birthdates.

5. Fill in the date of the court order for support and the termination date set by the judge (the eighteenth birthday of the youngest child being supported). Complete the information on the amount of current support to be paid, the amount of past due arrearage, if any, and the age of the arrearage (over twelve

weeks or not). Then fill in the correct pay period for the paying party.

6. Fill in the name of the circuit clerk and the address of that office, where the support checks will be sent.

7. If the Notice to Withhold Income for Child Support is to be served immediately on the employer, it should be sent by certified mail to the employer or personally delivered to the employer. The employer is required by Illinois law to comply with a Notice to Withhold Income for Child Support. Also be sure that your spouse receives a copy of the entered Notice to Withhold Income for Child Support.

8 Contested Divorce Procedure

Procedure Differences from Uncontested Divorce

This book cannot turn you into a trial lawyer. It can be very risky to handle a contested case yourself, although it has been done. There are several differences between a contested and an uncontested case. First, in an uncontested case the judge will usually go along with whatever you and your spouse have worked out. In a contested case you need to prove that you are entitled to what you are asking. This means you will need a longer time for the hearing, you will need to present papers as evidence, and you may need to have witnesses testify for you.

Second, you may have to do some extra work to get the evidence you need, such as by sending out subpoenas (which are discussed in the next section of this chapter), or even hiring a private investigator. Also, you will need to pay extra attention to assure that your spouse is properly notified of any court hearings, and that he or she is sent copies of any papers you file with the court clerk.

When it becomes apparent that you have a contested divorce, it is probably time to consider hiring an attorney, especially if the issue of child custody is involved. If you are truly ready to go to war over custody, it shows that this is an extremely important matter for you, and you may want to get professional assistance. You can predict a contested case when your spouse is seriously threatening to fight you every inch of the way, or when he or she hires an attorney.

On the other hand, you shouldn't assume that you need an attorney just because your spouse has hired one. Sometimes it will be easier to deal with the attorney than with your spouse. The attorney is not as emotionally involved and may see your settlement proposal as reasonable. So discuss things with your spouse's attorney first and see if things can be worked out. You can always hire your own lawyer if your spouse's isn't reasonable. Just be very cautious about signing any papers until you are certain you understand what they mean. You may want to have an attorney review any papers prepared by your spouse's lawyer before you sign them.

Aside from deciding if you want a lawyer, there are two main procedure differences between the uncontested and the contested divorce. First, you will need to be more prepared for the hearing. Second, you will not prepare the Judgment of Dissolution of Marriage (Form 20) until after the hearing with the judge. This is because you won't know what to put in the judgment until the judge decides the various matters in dispute.

The next chapters will discuss how to prepare for the issues to be argued at the hearing, and how to prepare the Judgment of Dissolution of Marriage.

Collecting Information

The judge will require a Financial Affidavit (Form 12) from you, and also one from your spouse. If your spouse has indicated that he or she will not cooperate at all, and will not provide a Financial Affidavit, you may have to try to get the information yourself. You can go to the hearing and tell the judge that your spouse won't cooperate, but the judge may just issue an order requiring your spouse to provide information (or be held in contempt of court), and continue the hearing to another date. It may help to speed things up if you are able to get the information yourself, and have it available at the hearing. This will require you to get subpoenas issued.

Before you send a subpoena to your spouse's employer, or bank, or accountant, you need to let your spouse know what you are about to do. The thought that you are about to get these other people involved in your divorce may be enough to get your spouse to cooperate. If your spouse calls and says "I'll give you the information," give him or her a few days to follow through. Ask when you can expect to receive the Financial Affidavit, and offer to send your spouse another blank copy if he or she needs one. If your spouse sends a completed Financial Affidavit as promised, don't send the subpoena. If your spouse doesn't follow through, go ahead with the subpoena. You can send out subpoenas to as many people or organizations as you need, but you'll need to use the following procedure for each subpoena.

Next, you will complete a form called Subpoena Duces Tecum (Form 22). This form will eventually be sent to whomever you want to supply you with information. Look at the Financial Affidavit form, and see what type of information is needed. If you were able to do a good job making copies of important papers while preparing to file for divorce, you should have the information you need to figure out where you need to send subpoenas. Your spouse's income information can be obtained from his or her employer. Stock and bond information can be obtained from his or her stock broker, bank account balances from the bank, auto loan balances from the lender, etc. You can have subpoenas issued to any or all of these places, but don't overdo it. Concentrate on income information (especially if you are asking for child support or expect to pay child support), and information on the major property items. And, it may not be necessary to send out subpoenas if you already have recent copies of the papers relating to these items. You can always show the judge the copies of your spouse's pay stubs, W-2 tax statements, or other papers at the hearing.

To complete the Subpoena Duces Tecum (Form 22) you need to:

1. Complete the top portion according to the instructions in chapter 5.

2. Type your spouse's employer's (or broker's, bank's, etc.) name and address after the word "To"

3. On the lines in the first paragraph, type in the number of the judicial circuit, name of the county, court location, courtroom number, and the time designated for the witnesses to produce the documents.

4. In the space after the words "purporting to be" type in a description of all documents needed for your spouse (e.g., all paychecks, bonuses, pension information, etc.). Be specific in identifying your spouse (such as giving full name and social security number), and in describing the documents requested.

5. On the two lines at the end of the main paragraph, type in the circuit court number (the same as the top of the page), and your name after the words "on the part of."

6. Type in your name, address, and phone number on the lines indicated at the bottom left corner of the form.

7. Leave the other spaces blank. Take the form to the court clerk and have the clerk fill out the rest of the spaces.

Next, mail a copy of the Subpoena Duces Tecum (Form 22), to your spouse.

Next, have the sheriff personally serve the Subpoena Duces Tecum to the person or place named in the subpoena. The sheriff will need at least one extra copy of the subpoena, and a check for the service fee. The employer, bank, etc., should send you the requested information. If the employer, bank, etc., calls you and says you must pay for copies, ask him how much they will cost and send a check or money order (if the amount isn't too high and you don't already have some fairly recent income information).

If the employer, bank, etc., doesn't provide the information, you can try sending a letter to the employer, bank, etc., saying: "unless you provide the information requested in the subpoena in 7 days, a motion for contempt may be filed with the circuit court." This may scare the employer, bank, etc., into sending you the information. The sheriff will have also filed an affidavit verifying when the subpoena was served. There are more procedures you could go through to force the employer, bank, etc., to give the information, but it probably isn't worth the hassle and you'd probably need an attorney to help you with it. At the final hearing you can tell the judge that your spouse refused to provide income information, and that the subpoena was not honored by the employer. The judge may do something to help you out, or he may advise you to see a lawyer.

There is also a procedure where you send written questions to your spouse, which he or she must answer in writing and under oath. These written questions are called *interrogatories*. If your spouse didn't file a Financial Affidavit, he or she probably won't answer the interrogatories either, which would leave you no better off. However, if you would like to try this, you may be able to locate the two forms you would need at the law library in one of the reference books previously mentioned (see the section on "Legal Research" in chapter 2).

Once you collect the information needed, you can prepare for the hearing.

Property and Debts

Generally, the judge will look at your property and debts, and will try to divide them fairly. This does not necessarily mean they will be divided fifty-fifty. What you want to do is offer the judge a reasonable solution that looks fair. Adultery or other misconduct on the part of one party may not be used to justify an unequal division of property and debts. A big difference in job earnings in a fairly long-term marriage (ten years or more) can be used to justify an unequal division.

It's time to review the Property Inventory (Form 1) and the Debt Inventory (Form 2) you prepared earlier. For each item or property, note which of the following categories it fits into (it may fit into more than one):

1. you really want.
2. you'd like to have.
3. you don't care either way.
4. your spouse really wants.
5. your spouse would like to have.
6. your spouse doesn't care either way.

Now start a list of what each of you should end up with, using the categories listed above. You will eventually end up with a list of things you can probably get with little difficulty (you really want and your spouse doesn't care), those which you'll fight over (you both really want), and those which need to be divided but can probably be easily divided equally (you both don't really care).

At the hearing the judge will probably urge you to work out your disagreements, but he won't put up with arguing for very long. In the end he will arbitrarily divide the items you can't agree upon, or he may order you to sell those items and divide the money you get equally.

On the few items that are really important to you it may be necessary for you to try to prove why you should get them. It will help if you can convince the judge of one or more of the following:

1. You paid for the item out of your own earnings or funds (though this makes no legal difference).
2. You are the one who primarily uses that item.

3. You use the item in your employment, business, or hobby.

4. You are willing to give something else you really want in exchange for that item. (Of course you will try to give up something from your "don't care" or your "like to have" list.)

5. The item is needed for your children (assuming you will have custody).

The best thing you can do is make a list of how you think the property should be divided. Make it a reasonably fair and equal list, regardless of how angry you are at your spouse. Even if the judge changes some of it to appear fair to your spouse, you will most likely get more of what you want than if you don't offer a suggestion. (No, this is not an exception to the negotiating rule of letting your spouse make the first offer, because at this point you are no longer just negotiating with your spouse. You are now negotiating with the judge. At this point you are trying to impress the judge with your fairness; not trying to convince your spouse.)

Special problems arise if a claim of nonmarital property becomes an issue. This may be in terms of your spouse trying to get your non-marital property, or in terms of you trying to get property you feel your spouse is wrongly claiming to be nonmarital. Basically, nonmarital property is property either of you had before you were married, and kept separate. (Refer to page 38; and Section 5/503 in appendix A, if you need to review marital and nonmarital property.)

It is also a good idea to have any papers proving that the property you claim to be nonmarital property is actually nonmarital property. These would be papers showing that:

- You bought the item before you were married (such as dated sales receipts).

- You inherited the item as your own property (such as certified copies of wills and probate court papers).

- You got the property by exchanging it for property you had before you got married, or for property you received as a gift or through an inheritance (such as a statement from the person you made the exchange with, or some kind of receipt showing what was exchanged).

If you want to get at assets your spouse is claiming are nonmarital assets, you will need to collect the following types of evidence:

- Papers showing that you helped pay for the asset (such as a check that you wrote, or bank statements showing that your money went into the same account that was used to make payments on the asset). For example, suppose your spouse purchased a house before you got married. During your marriage you made some of the mortgage payments with your own checking account (you will have cancelled checks, hopefully with the mortgage account number on them, to prove this). At other times, you deposited some of your paychecks into your spouse's checking account, and your spouse wrote checks from that account to pay the mortgage (again, there should be some bank records and cancelled checks that show this was done). Since you contributed to the purchase of the house, you can claim some of the value of the house as a marital asset.

- Papers showing that you paid for repairs of the asset. If you paid for repairs on the home, or a car your spouse had before you were married, you can claim part of the value.

- Papers showing that the asset was improved during your marriage. Example: Your spouse owned the house before you were married. During your marriage you and your spouse added a family room to the house. This will enable you to make a claim for some of the value of the house.

- Papers showing the asset was *commingled* (mixed) with marital assets or converted to joint tenancy property during the marriage.

In order to make a claim on what would otherwise appear to be your spouse's nonmarital property, you need to ask for it in your Petition for Dissolution of Marriage (Form 11). This is called a claim for a *special equity*. This means you will ask for it under *miscellaneous*, by describing the property item and claiming a marital interest in it. You will also need to list the asset in your Financial Affidavit. After the item is described, type in a short explanation of why you are entitled to the special equity. Generally this will be that you either (1) "have contributed to the purchase, repair or improvement of the property," or (2) that "the property has been commingled (mixed) with marital property" or "made joint property." The judge will have to look at whatever papers you show him, listen to what you and any witnesses will say about the situation, and decide if you are entitled to any of the value of the property.

During the hearing the judge will announce who gets which items. Make a list of this as the judge tells you. Then, complete the Judgment of Dissolution of Marriage (Form 20) according to what the judge says. Once you have completed the Judgment of Dissolution of Marriage, make a copy and send it to your spouse. Send the original to the judge or give it to the judge's personal clerk, along with a completed Proof of Service (Form 6) stapled to it showing the date you sent a copy to your spouse. If your spouse doesn't object to how you've prepared the judgment, the judge will sign the Judgment of Dissolution of Marriage and return a copy to you. You should send the judge the original and two copies of the Judgment of Dissolution of Marriage, along with two stamped envelopes (one addressed to yourself, and the other addressed to your spouse).

Child Custody and Visitation

Generally, if you are the wife, the odds start out in favor of you getting custody. But don't depend upon the odds. Start out by reviewing the guidelines the judge will use to decide the custody question. These can be found in chapter 4. For each item listed in that section, write down an explanation of how that item applies to you. This will be your argument when you have your hearing with the judge.

Many custody battles revolve around the moral fitness of one or both of the parents. If you become involved in this type of a custody fight, you should consult a lawyer. Charges of moral unfitness (such as illegal drug use, child abuse, immoral sexual conduct) can require long court hearings involving the testimony of many witnesses, as well as possibly the employment of private investigators. For such a hearing, you will require the help of an attorney who knows the law, what questions to ask witnesses, and the rules of evidence.

In many counties, if there is a custody battle, the parties will be ordered by the judge to go to mediation with professionals who try to help resolve the problem without a court hearing.

However, if the only question is whether you or your spouse have been the main caretaker of the child, you can always have friends, neighbors and relatives come into the hearing (if they are willing to help you) to testify on your behalf. And it may not be necessary for you to have an attorney. But, if you need to subpoena unwilling witnesses to testify, you should have an attorney.

The judge's decision regarding custody will have to be put into the Judgment of Dissolution of Marriage (Form 20). Read chapter 7 for instructions on preparing the Judgment of Dissolution of Marriage.

Child Support

In Illinois, as in most states, the question of child support is mostly a matter of a mathematical calculation. Getting a fair child support amount depends upon the accuracy of the income information presented to the judge. If you feel fairly sure that the information your spouse presents is accurate, or that you have obtained accurate information about his or her income, there isn't much to argue about. The judge will simply take the income information provided, use the formula to calculate the amount to be paid, and order that amount to be paid.

In most cases, there won't be much room to argue about the amount of child support, so there usually isn't a need to get an attorney. If you claim your spouse has not provided accurate income information, it will be up to you to prove this to the judge by showing the income information you have obtained from your spouse's employer or other source of income.

The only areas open for argument are whatever special needs are claimed by the party asking for child support. Once again, it will be necessary for that party to provide proof of the cost of these special needs by producing billing statements, receipts, or other papers to show the amount of these needs.

The judge's decision regarding child support will have to be put into the Judgment of Dissolution of Marriage (Form 20). Read chapter 7 for instructions on preparing the Judgment of Dissolution of Marriage.

Maintenance (Alimony)

A dispute over alimony may require a lawyer, especially if there is a request for permanent alimony because of a disability. Such a claim may require the testimony of expert witnesses (such as doctors, accountants, and actuaries), which requires the special knowledge of an attorney. A charge of adultery may also require a lawyer and possibly a private investigator as well.

If alimony has been requested, take a look at the Financial Affidavit (Form 12), or any other court papers asking for alimony, and review the reasons alimony was requested. These reasons will be the subject of the court hearing on this question. You should determine what information (including papers and the testimony of witnesses) you will need to present to the judge to either support or refute the reasons alimony was requested.

For short-term (also called *rehabilitative*) alimony, the most common reason is that the person needs help until he or she can get training to enter the work force. The questions that will need to be answered are:

1. What has the person been trained or educated for in the past?
2. What type of training or education is needed before the person can again be employable in that field?
3. How long will this training take?
4. What amount of income can be expected upon employment?
5. How much money is required for the training?

Questions that may be asked in either a temporary or a permanent alimony situation include an examination of the situation of the parties during their marriage that led to the person not working, what contribution to the marriage that person made, and what improper conduct on the part of the other party makes an award of alimony appropriate. You should be prepared to present evidence regarding these questions.

9 The Court Hearing

Preparation

Setting a Hearing Date

You will need to schedule a hearing date with the judge. See chapter 5 for instructions on setting a hearing date.

Notifying Your Spouse

You will need to notify your spouse of when the hearing will be. Even if you can call your spouse on the phone, it is a good idea to send a formal Notice (Form 5). Fill in the Notice according to the instructions in chapter 5. Then make three copies of the Notice. Mail one copy to your spouse, file the original with the court clerk, and keep two copies for yourself.

What Papers to Bring

Bring your copies (if available) of the following papers to the hearing:

- ☛ Your Petition for Dissolution of Marriage, and the affidavits you attached to it.
- ☛ Any papers you may have showing that your spouse was properly notified of the divorce (although the Sheriff's affidavit of serving papers will be in the court file, and you may not have a copy).
- ☛ Any papers you may have to support what is in your Financial Affidavit. This should include copies of your most recent pay stub, Federal income tax return, and W-2 forms.

- Any paper's showing your spouse's income or property.
- Your Marital Settlement Agreement, if you have one that hasn't yet been filed with the court.
- Your Judgment of Dissolution of Marriage (Form 9 or Form 20).
- A Certificate of Dissolution (obtained from clerk).

The Hearing

Your hearing will probably take place in a courtroom. It may look more like a conference room. Generally, the judge will be at the head of a table, with you and your spouse on either side. This may be the judge's *chambers* or office.

The judge may start the hearing by summarizing why you are there, then ask you and your spouse if you have any additional evidence to present, and then ask each of you any questions he may have. The judge will review the papers you filed with the clerk, and will probably ask you whether you understand and agree with what is in the papers. Because your ground for divorce is an "irretrievable breakdown of the marriage," the judge will also ask you to explain why your marriage is "irretrievably broken." Just tell him why you are getting divorced. (Example: "We just don't have any interests in common anymore, and have drifted apart," or "My husband has had several affairs.") You will probably be put under oath before answering these questions.

If you have any information that is different and more current than what is in the Financial Affidavits, you should mention to the judge that you have more current information. You will then give a copy of whatever papers you have to show the changed situation (such as current pay stub showing an increase in pay, or a current bank statement showing a new balance). The judge may ask to see any papers you have to prove what you've put in your Financial Affidavit. Your basic job at the hearing is to answer the judge's questions, and give him the information he needs to give you a divorce.

If there are any items that you and your spouse have not yet agreed upon, tell the judge about it. Refer to chapter 8, relating to the contested divorce, for more information about how to handle these unresolved issues. Be prepared to make a suggestion as to how these matters should be settled, and to explain to the judge why your suggestion is the best solution.

If the judge asks for any information that you haven't brought with you, tell the judge that you don't have it with you but you will be happy to provide him with the information by the end of the following day. Just be sure you get the papers to him!

At the end of the hearing the judge will tell you if he is going to grant you a divorce and accept your Marital Settlement Agreement. It would be unusual for him not to grant the divorce and accept your agreement. You will then tell the judge that you've prepared a proposed judgment, and hand him the original. Refer to chapter 7 regarding how to prepare the Judgment form. You should have two extra copies of the Judgment with you, one for yourself and one for your spouse. You should also bring two envelopes, one addressed to yourself and one addressed to your spouse, and two stamps. This is in case the judge wants to review the Judgment of Dissolution of Marriage and mail it to you later, instead of signing it at the hearing.

If the judge wants you to make any changes in the Judgment of Dissolution of Marriage, make a careful note of exactly what the judge wants (ask him to explain it again if you didn't understand the first time), then tell the judge that you will make the correction and deliver the judgment the following day. If the change requested is a small one, you might even be able to write in the change by hand at the hearing and initial the change.

If child support or alimony is to be paid, you will also need to bring an Order for Withholding (Form 21). The judge will sign the Order for

Withholding at the hearing. There will be copies for you, your spouse, the clerk, and the employer deducting the support.

When the hearing is over, thank the judge and leave. The judge will sign the original Judgment of Dissolution of Marriage, and send it to the court clerk's office to be entered in the court's file. Take the copies of the Judgment of Dissolution of Marriage, and Order for Withholding to the judge's clerk. She will write in the date and use a court seal on each copy to authenticate them. The petitioning party is responsible for giving a copy of the Order for Withholding to the employer. The party to receive support should always confirm that the employer received the Order for Withholding.

If any serious problems develop at the hearing (such as your spouse's attorney starts making a lot of technical objections, or the judge gives you a hard time), just tell the judge you'd like to continue the hearing so you can retain an attorney. Then go get one!

Child Support Agencies

There are two offices you need to be aware of:

Child Support Division of Circuit Clerk

This is the office that processes the child support and alimony payments. This is a division of the court clerk's office. The spouse responsible to pay the support (or his or her employer) will make payments here. The clerk then cashes that check and issues a check to the spouse entitled to receive support or alimony. This division keeps the official records of what has and has not been paid.

Illinois Department of Public Aid (IDPA)

The Child Support Enforcement office of the IDPA is responsible for enforcing the payment of child support to parents receiving welfare (Aid to Families with Dependent Children), and others who request their services. If you are to receive support and are receiving welfare benefits, you must contact your local Child Support Enforcement office. This office can also assist with collection in non-aid cases if you qualify for its enforcement assistance.

10 When You Can't Find Your Spouse

Your spouse has run off, and you have no idea of where he or she might be. Instead of personal service by the sheriff, you will use a method of giving notice called *service by publication*. You will need to carefully follow the steps listed below.

The Diligent Search

The court will only permit publication when you can't locate your spouse. This also includes the situation where the sheriff has made several attempts to serve your spouse, but it appears that your spouse is hiding to avoid being served. First, you'll have to show the court what you've done to try to find him or her. In making this search, try checking the following:

- phone book and directory assistance in the area where you live.
- directory assistance in the area where you last knew your spouse to be living.
- friends and relatives who might know where your spouse is living.

- the post office where he or she last lived to see if there is a forwarding address.
- records of the tax collector and property assessor to see if your spouse owns property.
- Department of Motor Vehicles to see if your spouse has any car registrations.
- any other sources you know that may lead you to a current address (such as landlords, prior employers, etc.).

If you find a current address, go back to personal service by the sheriff, but if not, continue with this procedure.

Preparing and Filing Court Papers

Once you have made your search you need to notify the court. This is done by filing the Affidavit for Service by Publication (Form 23). All this form does is tell the court what you've done to try to locate your spouse, and ask for permission to publish your notice. If your spouse lives in another state, and you do have his or her address, you may use this procedure. But since this is fairly complicated, you may want to call the sheriff in the county and state where your spouse lives and arrange for personal service by the sheriff. To complete the Affidavit for Service by Publication (Form 23) you need to:

1. Complete the top portion of the form according to the instructions in chapter 5.
2. Type your name in the blank at the beginning of the first paragraph.
3. Choose the appropriate line from paragraphs 1 and 2, and fill in the requested information, using the choices indicated by single or double asterisks.

4. Type in your name, address, and phone number below the notary public line.
5. Sign your name on the "Signature" line before a notary public.
6. File with the clerk.

You will also prepare a Notice by Publication (Form 24). File both forms with the clerk along with a self-addressed, stamped envelope. If the clerk finds any errors in your papers, he will notify you what needs to be corrected. To complete the Notice by Publication (Form 24):

1. Complete the top portion of the form according to the instructions in chapter 5.
2. Type your spouse's name in the blank in the first paragraph.
3. Fill in the address of the clerk's office, including the room number, in the second paragraph, and fill in a date for the required answer (to be safe, fill in a business day, not a weekend day, that is thirty-five days after the date you file this form).
4. Fill in your name, address, and telephone number.
5. File the notice with the clerk and deliver a copy to your local newspaper to be printed three times. Deliver it to the newspaper as soon as possible after filing it with the clerk.

Publishing

Your next step is to have a newspaper publish your Notice by Publication (Form 24). Check the yellow pages listings under "Newspapers," and call several of the smaller ones in your county (making sure it is in the same county as the court), and ask if they are approved for legal announcements. If they are, ask how much they charge to publish a Notice by Publication. You are searching for the cheapest paper. Most areas have a paper that specializes in the publishing of legal announcements, at a much cheaper rate than the regular daily newspapers. If you look around the courthouse you may be able to find a copy or newsstand for this paper.

Once you've found the paper you want, send them a copy of the Notice by Publication, along with the publication cover letter (Form 25). To complete Form 25, type in the date about fifteen lines down from the top of the page; type in the name and address of the newspaper just above the phrase "Dear Sir or Madam," then sign your name below the word "Sincerely," and type your name and address below your signature.

The Notice by Publication will be published once a week for three weeks. Get a copy of the paper the first time it will appear and check to be sure it was printed correctly. If you find an error, notify the newspaper immediately. As indicated in the Notice by Publication, your spouse has until a certain date to respond. If your spouse responds to the notice published in the newspaper, proceed with either the uncontested or contested procedure. If your spouse does not respond by the date stated in the Notice by Publication, proceed with the Motion to Enter Default (Form 18) (see chapter 7).

11 Special Circumstances

When You Can't Afford Court Costs

FORM 26

Application to Sue or Defend as a Poor Person (Form 26) is for use when you can't afford to pay the filing fee and other costs associated with the divorce. In order to qualify for a waiver of the filing fee, you must be *indigent*. If you are indigent, your income is probably low enough for you to qualify for public assistance (welfare).

> ***Caution:*** If you decide to use this form, you will probably be asked for more information to prove that you meet the requirements for being declared indigent, and therefore, eligible to have the filing and service fees waived. Before you file this form, you may want to see if the court clerk will give you any information on what is required to be declared indigent. You should also be aware that you can be held in contempt of court for giving false information on this form.

To complete the Application to Sue or Defend as a Poor Person (Form 26):

1. Complete the top portion according to the instructions in chapter 5.

2. After the words "County of," type in the name of the county in which you live (and where this form will be signed).

3. Fill in all information as to employment income and property.

4. If you are the petitioner, check "claim" in paragraph 7; if respondent, check "defense."

5. Sign the form before a notary, and file it with the clerk.

If the judge finds that you are not a "poor person," under the law, then you will be required to pay the costs to the clerk and sheriff in order to start the divorce process. The judge decides this by asking about your income, assets, debts, and employment.

Protecting Yourself, Your Children, and Your Property

Some people have three special concerns when preparing to file for divorce: Fear of physical attack by their spouse, fear that their spouse will take the children, and fear that their spouse will take property and hide it. There are additional legal papers you can file if you feel you are in any of these situations.

Protecting Yourself

If you or your children have suffered recent physical abuse, go immediately to the court clerk's office and ask to file a Petition for Domestic Violence Order of Protection. You will be assisted by the clerk and court personnel.

Protecting Your Children

If you are worried that your spouse may try to kidnap your children, you should make sure that the day care center, baby-sitter, relative, or whomever you leave the children with at any time, is aware that you are in the process of a divorce and that the children are only to be released to you personally (not to your spouse or to any other relative, friend, etc.). To prevent your spouse from taking the children out of the United States, you can apply for a passport for each child. Once a passport is issued, the government will not issue another. So get their passport and lock it in a safe deposit box. (This won't prevent them from being taken to Canada or Mexico, where passports are not required, but will prevent them from being taken overseas). You can also file a motion to prevent the removal of the children from the state. Forms for such other motions are discussed at the beginning of appendix B, in the section titled "Where to Find Additional Forms."

Protecting Your Property

If you genuinely fear that your spouse will try to remove money from bank accounts and try to hide important papers showing what property you own, you may want to take this same action before your spouse can. However, you can make a great deal of trouble for yourself with the judge if you do this to try to get these assets for yourself. So, make a complete list of any property you do take, and be sure to include these items in your Financial Affidavit (Form 12). You may need to convince the judge that you only took these items temporarily, in order to preserve them until a Judgment of Dissolution of Marriage is entered. Also, do not spend any cash you take from a bank account, or sell or give away any items of property you take.

Any cash should be placed in a separate bank account, without your spouse's name on it, and kept separate from any other cash you have. Any papers, such as deeds, car titles, stock or bond certificates, etc., should be placed in a safe deposit box, without your spouse's name on it. The idea is not to take these things for yourself, but to get them in a safe place so your spouse can't hide them and deny they ever existed.

There is no guaranteed way to prevent the things discussed in this chapter from happening. All you can do is put as many obstacles in his or her way as possible, and prepare for your spouse to suffer legal consequences for acting improperly.

Temporary Support and Custody

If your spouse has left you with the children, and the mortgage and monthly bills, and is not helping you out financially, you may want to consider asking the court to order the payment of support for you and the children during the divorce procedure. Of course, if you were the only person bringing in income and have been paying all the bills, don't expect to get any temporary support.

You will need to prepare a Petition for Temporary Relief (Form 27), and an Order for Temporary Support and Custody (Form 28). To complete the Petition for Temporary Relief (Form 27) you need to:

1. Complete the top portion of the form according to the instructions in chapter 5.
2. Fill in blanks and strike out portions that do not apply.
3. Type in the date and sign your name on the line at the bottom.
4. Attach copies of any of your spouse's pay stubs, most recent tax forms, or other information showing your spouse's income. You should have already filed your Financial Affidavit which will show your monthly expenses, as well as your income.

Call the judge's clerk and say that you would like to submit a Motion for Temporary Support to the judge, and ask how you should do this. The clerk may tell you to come in with your papers at a certain time, to mail them to the judge, or to submit them to the court clerk's office. Just follow the instructions. If possible, you should notify your spouse of your motion just before you go see the judge, either verbally or by mailing and filing a Proof of Service (Form 6). Otherwise, be prepared to tell the judge why you were unable to notify your spouse. To complete the Order for Temporary Support and Custody (Form 28), all you need to do is complete the top portion of the form. The judge will either fill in the rest, or tell you how to fill in the rest.

Once you have a signed copy of the Order for Temporary Support and Custody (Form 28), mail or deliver a copy to your spouse. Then complete a Proof of Service (Form 6) to show that you have notified your spouse. If your spouse has not filed any papers with the court yet, you should have the Order for Temporary Support and Custody served on him or her by the sheriff (refer back to chapter 6 for information on having papers served by the sheriff). It is important to be able to satisfy the judge that your spouse knew about the Order for Temporary Support and Custody if you need to collect support arrearages, or file contempt proceedings for violation of the custody order.

TAXES

As you are no doubt aware, the United States' income tax code is complicated and ever-changing. For this reason it is impossible to give detailed legal advice with respect to taxes in a book such as this. Any such information could easily be out of date by the time of publication. Therefore, it is strongly recommended that you consult your accountant, lawyer, or whomever prepares your tax return, about the tax consequences of a divorce. A few general concerns are discussed in this chapter, to give you an idea of some of the tax questions which can arise.

PROPERTY DIVISION AND TAXES

You and your spouse may be exchanging title to property as a result of your divorce. Generally, there will not be any tax to pay as the result of such a transfer. However, whomever gets a piece of property will be responsible to pay any tax which may become due upon sale.

The Internal Revenue Service (I.R.S.) has issued numerous rulings about how property is to be treated in divorce situations. You need to be especially careful if you are transferring any tax shelters, or other complicated financial arrangements.

Be sure to read the following section on alimony, because fancy property settlements are asking for tax problems.

Alimony and Taxes

Alimony can cause the most tax problems of any aspect of divorce. I.R.S. is always making new rulings on whether an agreement is really alimony, or is really property division. The basic rule is that alimony is treated as income to the person receiving it, and as a deduction for the person paying it. Therefore, in order to manipulate the tax consequences, many couples try to show something as part of the property settlement, instead of as alimony; or the reverse. As I.R.S. becomes aware of these "tax games" it issues rulings on how it will view a certain arrangement. If you are simply talking about the regular, periodic payment of cash, I.R.S. will probably not question that it is alimony. If you try to call it property settlement you may run into problems. The important thing is to consult a tax expert if you are considering any unusual or creative property settlement or alimony arrangements.

Child Support and Taxes

There are simple tax rules regarding child support:

1. Whoever has custody gets to claim the children on his or her tax return (unless both parents file a special I.R.S. form agreeing to a different arrangement each year).

2. The parent receiving child support does not need to report it as income.

3. The parent paying child support cannot deduct it.

If you are sharing physical custody, the parent with whom the child lives for the most time during the year is entitled to claim the child as a dependent, if there is no agreement or court order to the contrary. Keep in mind though that the judge in your case has the power to decide who claims children as dependents, along with custody and support.

The I.R.S. form to allow a variation form the IRS rule must be filed each year. Therefore, if you and your spouse have agreed that you will get to claim the children (even though you don't have custody), you should get your spouse to sign an open-ended form which you can file each year, so that you don't have to worry about it each year. A phone call to the I.R.S. can help you get answers to questions on this point.

Pension Plans

Pension plans, or retirement plans, of you and your spouse are marital assets. They may be valuable assets. If you and your spouse are young, and have not been working long, you may not have pension plans worth worrying about. Also, if you have both worked, and have similar pensions plans, it may be best just to include a provision in your settlement agreement that "each party shall keep his or her own pension plan." But if you have been married a long time, and your spouse worked while you stayed home to raise the children, your spouse's pension plan may be worth a lot of money, and may be necessary to see you through retirement. If you and your spouse cannot agree on how to divide a pension plan, you should see an attorney. The valuation of pension plans, and how they are to be divided, is a complicated matter which you should not attempt.

If Your Spouse Also Filed for Divorce

If your spouse filed for divorce first, you need to respond in writing within twenty days of receiving the summons and Petition for Dissolution of Marriage. You can use Form 13, but this will basically admit what your spouse is asking for in his or her Petition for Dissolution of Marriage. You should specifically deny the parts of your spouse's petition in which you are in disagreement. If you feel that you are in over your head, see a lawyer.

File your Response to Petition for Dissolution of Marriage with the clerk. You will also need to mail a copy to your spouse, and complete and file a Proof of Service (Form 6) to show the court that copies were mailed.

If you filed for divorce first, but your spouse then filed a response and counter petition, you will need to file a Response to Petition for Dissolution of Marriage (Form 13).

APPENDIX A
ILLINOIS STATUTES

This appendix contains selected portions of Chapter 750 of the Illinois Compiled Statues (State Bar Association Edition). For a complete understanding of the law, it is suggested that you visit you public library or law library and review *all* of Chapter 750.

5/401. Dissolution of marriage

Sec. 401. Dissolution of marriage.

(a) The court shall enter judgment of dissolution of marriage if at the time the action was commenced one of the spouses was a resident of this State or was stationed in this State while a member of the armed services, and the residence or military presence had been maintained for 90 days next preceding the commencement of the action or the making of the finding; provided, however, that a finding of residence of a party in any judgment entered under this Act from January 1, 1982 through June 30, 1982 shall satisfy the former domicile requirements of this Act; and if one of the following grounds for dissolution has been proved:

(1) That, without cause or provocation by the petitioner: the respondent was at the time of such marriage, and continues to be naturally impotent; the respondent had a wife or husband living at the time of the marriage; the respondent had committed adultery subsequent to the marriage; the respondent has wilfully deserted or absented himself or herself from the petitioner for the space of one year, including any period during which litigation may have pended between the spouses for dissolution of marriage or legal separation; the respondent has been guilty of habitual drunkenness for the space of 2 years; the respondent has been guilty of gross and confirmed habits caused by the excessive use of addictive drugs for the space of 2 years, or has attempted the life of the other by poison or other means showing malice, or has been guilty of extreme and repeated physical or mental cruelty, or has been convicted of a felony or other infamous crime; or the respondent has infected the other with a communicable venereal disease. "Excessive use of addictive drugs", as used in this Section, refers to use of an addictive drug by a person when using the drug becomes a controlling or a dominant purpose of his life; or

(2) That the spouses have lived separate and apart for a continuous period in excess of 2 years and irreconcilable differences have caused the irretrievable breakdown of the marriage and the court determines that efforts at reconciliation have failed or that future attempts at reconciliation would be impracticable and not in the best interests of the family. If the spouses have lived separate and apart for a continuous period of not less than 6 months next preceding the entry of the judgment dissolving the marriage, as evidenced by

testimony or affidavits of the spouses, the requirement of living separate and apart for a continuous period in excess of 2 years may be waived upon written stipulation of both spouses filed with the court. At any time after the parties cease to cohabit, the following periods shall be included in the period of separation:

(A) any period of cohabitation during which the parties attempted in good faith to reconcile and participated in marriage counseling under the guidance of any of the following: a psychiatrist, a clinical psychologist, a clinical social worker, a marriage and family therapist, a person authorized to provide counseling in accordance with the prescriptions of any religious denomination, or a person regularly engaged in providing family or marriage counseling; and

(B) any period of cohabitation under written agreement of the parties to attempt to reconcile.

In computing the period during which the spouses have lived separate and apart for purposes of this Section, periods during which the spouses were living separate and apart prior to July 1, 1984 are included.

(b) Judgment shall not be entered unless, to the extent it has jurisdiction to do so, the court has considered, approved, reserved or made provision for child custody, the support of any child of the marriage entitled to support, the maintenance of either spouse and the disposition of property. The court may enter a judgment for dissolution that reserves any of these issues either upon (i) agreement of the parties, of (ii) motion of either party and a finding by the court that appropriate circumstances exist.

The death of a party subsequent to entry of a judgment for dissolution but before judgment on reserved issues shall not abate the proceedings.

If any provision of this Section or its application shall be adjudged unconstitutional or invalid for any reason by any court of competent jurisdiction, that judgment shall not impair, affect or invalidate any other provision or application of this Section, which shall remain in full force and effect.

5/402. Legal separation

Sec. 402. Legal Separation.

(a) Any person living separate and apart from his or her spouse without fault may have a remedy for reasonable support and maintenance while they so live apart.

(b) Such action shall be brought in the circuit court of the county in which the respondent resides or in which the parties last resided together as husband and wife. In the event the respondent cannot be found within the State, the action may be brought in the circuit court of the county in which the petitioner resides. Commencement of the action, temporary relief and trials shall be the same as in actions for dissolution of marriage.

(c) A proceeding or judgment for legal separation shall not bar either party from instituting an action for dissolution of marriage, and if the party so moving has met the requirements of Section 401, a judgment for dissolution shall be granted.

5/503. Disposition of property

Sec. 503. Disposition of property.

(a) For purposes of this Act, "marital property" means all property acquired by either spouse subsequent to the marriage, except the following, which is known as "non-marital property":

(1) property acquired by gift, legacy or descent;

(2) property acquired in exchange for property acquired before the marriage or in exchange for property acquired by gift, legacy or descent;

(3) property acquired by a spouse after a judgment of legal separation;

(4) property excluded by valid agreement of the parties;

(5) any judgment or property obtained by judgment awarded to a spouse from the other spouse;

(6) property acquired before the marriage;

(7) the increase in value of property acquired by a method listed in paragraphs (1) through (6) of this subsection, irrespective of whether the increase results from a contribution of marital property, non-marital property, the personal effort of a spouse, or otherwise, subject to the right of reimbursement provided in subsection (c) of this Section; and

(8) income from property acquired by a method listed in paragraphs (1) through (7) of this subsection if the income is not attributable to the personal effort of a spouse.

(b) For purposes of distribution of property pursuant to this Section, all property acquired by either spouse after the marriage and before a judgment of dissolution of marriage or declaration of invalidity of marriage, including non-marital property transferred into some form of co-ownership between the spouses, is presumed to be marital property, regardless of whether title is held individually or by the spouses in some form of co-ownership such as joint tenancy, tenancy in common, tenancy by the entirety, or community property. The presumption of marital property is overcome by a showing that the property was acquired by a method listed in subsection (a) of this Section.

(c) Commingled marital and non-marital property shall be treated in the following manner, unless otherwise agreed by the spouses:

(1) When marital and non-marital property are commingled by contributing one estate of property into another resulting in a loss of identity of the contributed property, the classification of the contributed property is transmuted to the estate receiving the contribution, subject to the provisions of paragraph (2) of this subsection; provided that if marital and non-marital property are commingled into newly acquired property resulting in a loss of identity of the contributing estates, the commingled property shall be deemed transmuted to marital property, subject to the provisions of paragraph (2) of this subsection.

(2) When one estate of property makes a contribution to another estate of property, or when a spouse contributes personal effort to non-marital property, the contributing estate shall be reimbursed from the estate receiving the contribution notwithstanding any transmutation; provided, that no such reimbursement shall be made with respect to a contribution which is not retraceable by clear and convincing evidence, or was a gift, or, in the case of a contribution of personal effort of a spouse to non-marital property, unless the effort is significant and results in substantial appreciation of the non-marital property. Personal effort of a spouse shall be deemed a contribution by the marital estate. The court may provide for reimbursement out of the marital property to be divided or by imposing a lien against the non-marital property which received the contribution.

(d) In a proceeding for dissolution of marriage or declaration of invalidity of marriage, or in a proceeding for disposition of property following dissolution of marriage by a court which lacked personal jurisdiction over the absent spouse or lacked jurisdiction to dispose of the property, the court shall assign each spouse's non-marital property to that spouse. It also shall divide the marital property without regard to marital misconduct in just proportions considering all relevant factors, including:

(1) the contribution of each party to the acquisition, preservation, or increase or decrease in value of the marital or non-marital property, including the contribution of a spouse as a homemaker or to the family unit;

(2) the dissipation by each party of the marital or non-marital property;

(3) the value of the property assigned to each spouse;

(4) the duration of the marriage;

(5) the relevant economic circumstances of each spouse when the division of property is to become effective, including the desirability of awarding the family home, or the right to live therein for reasonable periods, to the spouse having custody of the children;

(6) any obligations and rights arising from a prior marriage of either party;

(7) any antenuptial agreement of the parties;

(8) the age, health, station, occupation, amount and sources of income, vocational skills, employability, estate, liabilities, and needs of each of the parties;

(9) the custodial provisions for any children;

(10) whether the apportionment is in lieu of or in addition to maintenance;

(11) the reasonable opportunity of each spouse for future acquisition of capital assets and income; and

(12) the tax consequences of the property division upon the respective economic circumstances of the parties.

(e) Each spouse has a species of common ownership in the marital property which vests at the time dissolution proceedings are commenced and continues only during the pendency of the action. Any such interest in marital property shall not encumber that property so as to restrict its transfer, assignment or conveyance by the title holder unless such title holder is specifically enjoined from making such transfer, assignment or conveyance.

(f) In a proceeding for dissolution of marriage or declaration of invalidity of marriage or in a proceeding for disposition of property following dissolution of marriage by a court that lacked personal jurisdiction over the absent spouse or lacked jurisdiction to dispose of the property, the court, in determining the value of the marital and non-marital property for purposes of dividing the property, shall value the property as of the date of trial or some other date as close to the date of trial as is practicable.

(g) The court if necessary to protect and promote the best interests of the children may set aside a portion of the jointly or separately held estates of the parties in a separate fund or trust for the support, maintenance, education, and general welfare of any minor, dependent, or incompetent child of the parties. In making a determination under this subsection, the court may consider, among other things, the conviction of a party of any of the offenses set forth in Section 12-4, 12-4.1, 12-4.2, 12-4.3, 12-13, 12-14, 12-14.1, 12-15, or 12-16 of the Criminal Code of 1961 if the victim is a child of one or both of the parties, and there is a need for, and cost of, care, healing and counseling for the child who is the victim of the crime.

(h) Unless specifically directed by a reviewing court, or upon good cause shown, the court shall not on remand consider any increase or decrease in the value of any "marital" or "non-marital" property occurring since the assessment of such property at the original trial or hearing, but shall use only that assessment made at the original trial or hearing.

(i) The court may make such judgments affecting the marital property as may be just and may enforce such judgments by ordering a sale of marital property, with proceeds therefrom to be applied as determined by the court.

(j) After proofs have closed in the final hearing on all other issues between the parties (or in conjunction with the final hearing, if all parties so stipulate) and before judgment is entered, a party's petition for contribution to fees and costs incurred in the proceeding shall be heard and decided, in accordance with the following provisions:

(1) A petition for contribution, if not filed before the final hearing on other issues between the parties, shall be filed no later than 30 days after the closing of proofs in the final hearing or within such other period as the court orders.

(2) Any award of contribution to one party from the other party shall be based on the criteria for division of marital property under this Section 503 and, if maintenance has been awarded, on the criteria for an award of maintenance under Section 504.

(3) The filing of a petition for contribution shall not be deemed to constitute a waiver of the attorney-client privilege between the petitioning party and current or former counsel; and such a waiver shall not constitute a prerequisite to a hearing for contribution. If either party's presentation on contribution, however, includes evidence within the scope of the attorney-client privilege, the disclosure or disclosures shall be narrowly construed and shall not be deemed by the court to constitute a general waiver of the privilege as to matters beyond the scope of the presentation.

(4) No finding on which a contribution award is based or denied shall be asserted against counsel or former counsel for purposes of any hearing under subsection (c) or (e) of Section 508.

(5) A contribution award (payable to either the petitioning party or the party's counsel, or jointly, as the court determines) may be in the form of either a set dollar amount or a percentage of fees and costs (or a portion of fees and costs) to be subsequently agreed upon by the petitioning party and counsel or, alternatively, thereafter determined in a hearing pursuant to subsection (c) of Section 508 or previously or thereafter determined in an independent proceeding under subsection (e) of Section 508.

(6) The changes to this Section 503 made by this amendatory Act of 1996 apply to cases pending on or after June 1, 1997, Except as otherwise provided in Section 508.

5/504. Maintenance

Sec. 504. Maintenance.

(a) In a proceeding for dissolution of marriage or legal separation or declaration of invalidity of marriage, or a proceeding for maintenance following dissolution of the marriage by a court which lacked personal jurisdiction over the absent spouse, the court may grant a temporary or permanent maintenance award for either spouse in amounts and for periods of time as the court deems just, without regard to marital misconduct, in gross or for fixed or indefinite periods of time, and the maintenance may be paid from the income or property of the other spouse after consideration of all relevant factors, including:

(1) the income and property of each party, including marital property apportioned and non-marital property assigned to the party seeking maintenance;

(2) the needs of each party;

(3) the present and future earning capacity of each party;

(4) any impairment of the present and future earning capacity of the party seeking maintenance due to that party devoting time to domestic duties or having foregone or delayed education, training, employment, or career opportunities due to the marriage;

(5) the time necessary to enable the party seeking maintenance to acquire appropriate education, training, and employment, and whether that party is able to support himself or herself through appropriate employment or is the custodian of a child making it appropriate that the custodian not seek employment;

(6) the standard of living established during the marriage;

(7) the duration of the marriage;

(8) the age and the physical and emotional condition of both parties;

(9) the tax consequences of the property division upon the respective economic circumstances of the parties;

(10) contributions and services by the party seeking maintenance to the education, training, career or career potential, or license of the other spouse;

(11) any valid agreement of the parties; and

(12) any other factor that the court expressly finds to be just and equitable.

(c) The court may grant and enforce the payment of maintenance during the pendency of an appeal as the court shall deem reasonable and proper.

(d) No maintenance shall accrue during the period in which a party is imprisoned for failure to comply with the court's order for the payment of such maintenance.

(e) When maintenance is to be paid through the clerk of the court in a county of 1,000,000 inhabitants or less, the order shall direct the obligor to pay to the clerk, in addition to the maintenance payments, all fees imposed by the county board under paragraph (3) of subsection (u) of Section 27.1 of the Clerks of Courts Act. Unless paid in cash or pursuant to an order for withholding, the payment of the fee shall be by a separate instrument from the support payment and shall be made to the order of the Clerk.

5/505. Child support-Contempt-Penalties

Sec. 505. Child support; contempt; penalties.

(a) In a proceeding for dissolution of marriage, legal separation, declaration of invalidity of marriage, a proceeding for child support following dissolution of the marriage by a court which lacked personal jurisdiction over the absent spouse, a proceeding for modification of a previous order for child support under Section 510 of this Act, or any proceeding authorized under Section 501 or 601 of this Act, the court may order either or both parents owing a duty of support to a child of the marriage to pay an amount reasonable and necessary for his support, without regard to marital misconduct. The duty of support owed to a minor child includes the obligation to provide for the reasonable and necessary physical, mental and emotional health needs of the child.

(1) The Court shall determine the minimum amount of support by using the following guidelines:

Number of Children	Percent of Supporting Party's Net Income
1	20%
2	25%
3	32%
4	40%
5	45%
6 or more	50%

(2) The above guidelines shall be applied in each case unless the court makes a finding that application of the guidelines would be inappropriate, after considering the best interests of the child in light of evidence including but not

limited to one or more of the following relevant factors:

(A) the financial resources of the child;

(B) the financial resources and needs of the custodial parent;

(C) the standard of living the child would have enjoyed had the marriage not been dissolved;

(D) the physical and emotional condition of the child, and his educational needs; and

(E) the financial resources and needs of the non-custodial parent.

If the court deviates from the guidelines, the court's finding shall state the amount of support that would have been required under the guidelines, if determinable. The court shall include the reason or reasons for the variance from the guidelines.

(3) "Net income" is defined as the total of all income from all sources, minus the following deductions:

(A) Federal income tax (properly calculated withholding or estimated payments);

(B) State income tax (properly calculated withholding or estimated payments);

(C) Social Security (FICA payments);

(D) Mandatory retirement contributions required by law or as a condition of employment;

(E) Union dues;

(F) Dependent and individual health/hospitalization insurance premiums;

(G) Prior obligations of support or maintenance actually paid pursuant to a court order;

(H) Expenditures for repayment of debts that represent reasonable and necessary expenses for the production of income, medical expenditures necessary to preserve life or health, reasonable expenditures for the benefit of the child and the other parent, exclusive of gifts. The court shall reduce net income in determining the minimum amount of support to be ordered only for the period that such payments are due and shall enter an order containing provisions for its self-executing modification upon termination of such payment period.

(4) In cases where the court order provides for health/hospitalization insurance coverage pursuant to Section 505.2 of this Act, the premiums for that insurance, or that portion of the premiums for which the supporting party is responsible in the case of insurance provided through an employer's health insurance plan where the employer pays a portion of the premiums, shall be subtracted from net income in determining the minimum amount of support to be ordered.

(4.5) In a proceeding for child support following dissolution of the marriage by a court that lacked personal jurisdiction over the absent spouse, and in which the court is requiring payment of support for the period before the date an order for current support is entered, there is a rebuttable presumption that the supporting party's net income for the prior period was the same as his or her net income at the time the order for current support is entered.

(5) If the net income cannot be determined because of default or any other reason, the court shall order support in an amount considered reasonable in the particular case. The final order in all cases shall state the support level in dollar amounts.

(b) Failure of either parent to comply with an order to pay support shall be punishable as in other cases of contempt. In addition to other penalties provided by law the Court may, after finding the parent guilty of contempt, order that the parent be:

(1) placed on probation with such conditions of probation as the Court deems advisable;

(2) sentenced to periodic imprisonment for a period not to exceed 6 months; provided, however, that the Court may permit the parent to be released for periods of time during the day or night to:

(A) work; or

(B) conduct a business or other self-employed occupation.

The Court may further order any part or all of the earnings of a parent during a sentence of periodic imprisonment paid to the Clerk of the Circuit Court or to the parent having custody or to the guardian having custody of the minor children of the sentenced parent for the support of said minor children until further order of the Court.

(c) A one-time charge of 20% is imposable upon the amount of past-due child support owed on July 1, 1988 which has accrued under a support order entered by the court. The charge shall be imposed in accordance with the provisions of Section 10-21 of the Illinois Public Aid Code and shall be enforced by the court upon petition.

(d) Any new or existing support order entered by the court under this Section shall be deemed to be a series of judgments against the person obligated to pay support thereunder, each such judgment to be in the amount of each payment or installment of support and each such judgment to be deemed entered as of the date the corresponding payment or installment becomes due under the terms of the support order. Each such judgment shall have the full force, effect and attributes of any other judgment of this State, including the ability to be enforced.

(e) When child support is to be paid through the clerk of the court in a county of 1,000,000 inhabitants or less, the order shall direct the obligor to pay to the clerk, in addition to the child support payments, all fees imposed by the county board under paragraph (3) of subsection (u) of Section 27.1 of the Clerks of Courts Act. Unless paid in cash or pursuant to an order for withholding, the payment of the fee shall be by a separate instrument from the support payment and shall be made to the order of the Clerk.

(f) An order for support entered or modified in a case in which a party is receiving child and spouse support services under Article X of the Illinois Public Aid Code shall include a provision requiring the obligor to notify the Illinois Department of Public Aid, within 7 days, (i) of the name and address of any new employer of the obligor, (ii) whether the obligor has access to health insurance coverage through the employer or other group coverage, and (iii) if so, the policy name and number and the names of persons covered under the policy.

(g) An order for support shall include a date on which the current support obligation terminates. The termination date shall be no earlier than the date on which the child covered by the order will attain the age of majority or is otherwise emancipated. The order for support shall state that the termination date does not apply to any arrearage that may remain unpaid on that date. Nothing in this subsection shall be construed to prevent the court from modifying the order.

5/602. Best interest of child

Sec. 602. Best Interest of Child.

(a) The court shall determine custody in accordance with the best interest of the child. The court shall consider all relevant factors including:

(1) the wishes of the child's parent or parents as to his custody;

(2) the wishes of the child as to his custodian;

(3) the interaction and interrelationship of the child with his parent or parents, his siblings and any other person who may significantly affect the child's best interest;

(4) the child's adjustment to his home, school and community;

(5) the mental and physical health of all individuals involved;

(6) the physical violence or threat of physical violence by the child's potential custodian, whether directed against the child or directed against another person;

(7) the occurrence of ongoing abuse as defined in Section 103 of the Illinois Domestic Violence Act of 1986 whether directed against the child or directed against another person; and

(8) the willingness and ability of each parent to facilitate and encourage a close and continuing relationship between the other parent and the child.

(b) The court shall not consider conduct of a present or proposed custodian that does not affect his relationship to the child.

(c) Unless the court finds the occurrence of ongoing abuse as defined in Section 103 of the Illinois Domestic Violence Act of 1986, the court shall presume that the maximum involvement and cooperation of both parents regarding the physical, mental, moral, and emotional well-being of their child is in the best interest of the child. There shall be no presumption in favor of or against joint custody.

5/602.1 Parental powers-Joint custody-Criteria

Sec. 602.1.

(a) The dissolution of marriage, the declaration of invalidity of marriage, the legal separation of the parents, or the parents living separate and apart shall not diminish parental powers, rights, and responsibilities except as the court for good reason may determine under the standards of Section 602.

(b) Upon the application of either or both parents, or upon its own motion, the court shall consider an award of joint custody. Joint custody means custody determined pursuant to a Joint Parenting Agreement or a Joint Parenting Order. In such cases, the court shall initially request the parents to produce a Joint Parenting Agreement. Such Agreement shall specify each parent's powers, rights and responsibilities for the personal care of the child and for major decisions such as education, health care, and religious training. The Agreement shall further specify a procedure by which proposed changes, disputes and alleged breaches may be mediated or otherwise resolved and shall provide for a periodic review of its terms by the parents. In producing a Joint Parenting Agreement, the parents shall be flexible in arriving at resolutions which further the policy of this State as expressed in Sections 102 and 602. For the purpose of assisting the court in making a determination whether an award of joint custody is appropriate, the court may order mediation and may direct that an investigation be conducted pursuant to the provisions of Section 605. In the event the parents fail to produce a Joint Parenting Agreement, the court may enter an appropriate Joint Parenting Order under the standards of Section 602 which shall specify and contain the same elements as a Joint parenting Agreement, or it may award sole custody under the standards of Sections 602, 607, and 608.

(c) The court may enter an order of joint custody if it determines that joint custody would be in the best interest of the child, taking into account the following:

(1) the ability of the parents to cooperate effectively and consistently in matters that directly affect the joint parenting of the child. "Ability of the parents to cooperate" means the parents' capacity to substantially comply with a Joint Parenting Order. The court shall not consider the inability of the parents to cooperate effectively and consistently in matters that do not directly affect the joint parenting of the child;

(2) The residential circumstances of each parent; and

(3) all other factors which may be relevant to the best interest of the child.

(d) Nothing within this section shall imply or presume that joint custody shall necessarily mean equal parenting time. The physical residence of the child in joint custodial situations shall be determined by:

(1) express agreement of the parties; or

(2) order of the court under the standards of this Section.

(e) Notwithstanding any other provision of law, access to records and information pertaining to a child, including but not limited to medical, dental, child care and school records, shall not be denied to a parent for the reason that such parent is not the child's custodial parent; however, no parent shall have access to the school records of a child if the parent is prohibited by an order of protection from inspecting or obtaining such records pursuant to the Illinois Domestic Violence Act of 1986, as now or hereafter amended.

Appendix B
Forms

Be sure to read the section "An Introduction to Legal Forms" in chapter 5 before you begin using the forms in this appendix. Instructions for completing these forms are found throughout this book. The instructions for a particular form may be found by looking in the index under the heading "forms, instructions." You will not need to use all of the forms in this appendix.

Do not remove the forms from this appendix. Instead, make photocopies to use for both practice worksheets and the forms you will actually file with the court. This way you will still have the blank forms in this appendix to make more copies in the event you make mistakes or need additional copies.

Where to Find Additional Forms

This book is designed for the most typical divorce situations. In unusual situations there are numerous other forms that can be filed to obtain various results. There are two basic sources of legal forms. The first is the law library. Ask the librarian where to find divorce form books. (See the section on "Legal Research" in chapter 2.)

A second source will be the forms published by the Illinois Bar Association in various books. Check with the court clerk and the law library to see where and how you can get these forms. These will include forms for protection against domestic violence, ordering drug testing, the appointment of a guardian ad litem for the children, counselling and psychological examinations, mediation, prevention of removal of the children from the state, and dismissing a divorce case due to a reconciliation with your spouse.

Table of Forms

PROPERTY INVENTORY

(1) N-M	(2) DESCRIPTION	(3) ID#	(4) VALUE	(5) BALANCE OWED	(6) EQUITY	(7) OWNER H-W-J	(8) H	(9) W

Form 2

DEBT INVENTORY

(1) N-M	(2) CREDITOR	(3) ACCOUNT NO.	(4) NOTES	(5) MONTHLY PAYMENT	(6) BALANCE OWED	(7) DATE	(8) OWNER H-W-J	(9) H	(10) W

CHILD SUPPORT CALCULATION METHOD

Actual Monthly Gross Income from all sources $________________

Deductions (Monthly):

a) Federal Income Tax $________________

b) State Income Tax $________________

c) FICA (Social Security) $________________

d) Mandatory (not voluntary) pension/retirement contributions $________________

e) Union dues $________________

f) Health/hospitalization insurance premiums (self and dependents) $________________

g) Child support or maintenance payments required by prior court orders $________________

h) Reasonable and necessary business expenses for the production of income $________________

i) Medical expenses actually owing which are necessary to preserve life or health $________________

j) Special needs expenses for the child(ren), e.g., special education, therapy, etc. $________________

ACTUAL MONTHLY NET INCOME $________________

Multiply Actual Monthly Net Income by minimum statutory percentage for actual number of children of marriage:

ACTUAL NET	x 20% (one child) =	$________________ *
	x 25% (two children) =	$________________
	x 32% (three children) =	$________________
	x 40% (four children) =	$________________
	x 45% (five children) =	$________________
	x 50% (six children) =	$________________

*** This is the minimum child support (usually the actual amount ordered as well) to be paid by the non-custodial parent. The Order for Withholding with this amount filled in as the amount "for current support" (see Form 21).**

IN THE CIRCUIT COURT OF THE ______________________ JUDICIAL
CIRCUIT, IN AND FOR ______________________ COUNTY, ILLINOIS

IN RE: The Marriage of

_____________________________________,
Petitioner,

and

No.___________________

_____________________________________,
Respondent.

MOTION TO SET HEARING

The Petitioner moves this Honorable Court to set a hearing on the Petition for Dissolution of Marriage filed herein, on a date certain.

____
Petitioner (signature)

Name: ___________________________

Address: ___________________________

____

Telephone: ___________________________

IN THE CIRCUIT COURT OF THE ______________________ JUDICIAL
CIRCUIT, IN AND FOR ________________________ COUNTY, ILLINOIS

IN RE: The Marriage of

______________________________________,
Petitioner,

and No.__________________

______________________________________,
Respondent.

NOTICE

TO:

YOU ARE HEREBY NOTIFIED that on the ______ day of ____________________, ___________, at ___________o'clock ________.m., or as soon thereafter as counsel may be heard, I shall appear before the Honorable Judge ______________________________, in the room occupied by h_____ as a courtroom at the ______________________________ ____, Illinois, for hearing on Petition for Dissolution of Marriage and Entry of Judgment of Dissolution, at which time and place you may appear if you so desire.

____
Signature

Name:____________________________

Address:__________________________
____

Telephone:________________________

IN THE CIRCUIT COURT OF THE ______________________ JUDICIAL
CIRCUIT, IN AND FOR ________________________ COUNTY, ILLINOIS

IN RE: The Marriage of

______________________________________,

Petitioner,

and

No.__________________

______________________________________,

Respondent.

PROOF OF SERVICE

The undersigned certifies that a copy of the foregoing ________________________ ____ was/were served upon the following, by enclosing same in an envelope addressed to ________________ ______________________________ at _______ last known addresses, with postage fully prepaid, and by depositing said envelope in a U.S. Post Office Box in __________________, Illinois, on the ________ day of______________________, ________.

____

Signature

Subscribed and sworn to before me this
_____ day of ______________, ______.

____

Notary Public

IN THE CIRCUIT COURT OF THE ______________________ JUDICIAL
CIRCUIT, IN AND FOR ______________________ COUNTY, ILLINOIS

IN RE: The Marriage of

______________________________,
Petitioner,

and

No.______________

______________________________,
Respondent.

JOINT PETITION FOR SIMPLIFIED DISSOLUTION OF MARRIAGE

Now come Petitioner, ______________________________, without counsel, and
(Type or Print Petitioner's Name)

Respondent, ______________________________, without counsel, hereby petition this
(Type or Print Respondent's Name)
Honorable Court for a dissolution of the marriage between Petitioner and Respondent. In support of this petition for dissolution of marriage, the parties state as follows:

1. The Petitioner is presently ____ years of age; Petitioner's occupation is ______________________;

   Petitioner resides at ______________________, ______________________, Illinois;
   (Street Address) (City)
   and [ ] has [ ] has not resided in the State of Illinois for at least ninety (90) days immediately preceding the
   (Check one)
   filing of this Petition for Dissolution of Marriage.

2. The Respondent is presently ____ years of age; Respondent's occupation is______________________;

   Respondent resides at ______________________, ______________________, Illinois;
   (Street Address) (City)
   and [ ] has [ ] has not resided in the State of Illinois for at least ninety (90) days immediately preceding the
   (Check one)
   filing of this Petition for Dissolution of Marriage.

3. The Petitioner and Respondent have been married for less than five (5) years prior to the filing of this petition;

   they were married on ______________, ______; in______________________ County,
   (Month) (Day) (Year) (County)

   ______________________.
   (State)

4. No children were born to the parties during their relationship; no children were adopted by the parties; and

   ______________________________, to her knowledge, is not pregnant.
   (Type or Print Wife's Name)

5. The parties have lived separate and apart for a continuous period in excess of six (6) months and irreconcilable differences have caused the irretrievable breakdown of their marriage; efforts at reconciliation have failed and future attempts at reconciliation would be impracticable and not in the best interests of

the parties. The parties have signed an affidavit waiving the requirement for a continuous period living separate and apart in excess of two (2) years. The parties have lived separate and apart since ____________________________, _________.

6. Neither party is dependent on the other party for spousal support (also known as alimony or maintenance), or each party is willing to waive the right to spousal support. Both parties understand that consulting with attorneys may help determine eligibility for spousal support. Both parties waive any rights to maintenance.
7. Neither party has any interest in real property (real estate).
8. The parties have disclosed to each other all assets and their tax returns for all years of the marriage.
9. Petitioner's gross annual income from all sources is $_____________, and Respondent's gross annual income from all sources is $_____________, and the total annual income of the parties is less than $25,000.00.
10. The total fair market value of all marital property, after deducting all encumbrances, is less than $5,000.00 and the parties have executed a written agreement dividing all assets in excess of $100.00 in value and allocating responsibility for debts and liabilities between the parties. A copy of the written agreement, Signed by both parties, filed with this petition.
11. (Optional) ____'s former/maiden name was
    (Type or Print Wife's Name)
    ____.
    (Type or Print Wife's Maiden OR Former Name)

WHEREFORE, the parties pray as follows:

A. That the parties be awarded a Judgment of Dissolution of Marriage dissolving the bonds of matrimony existing between them.

B. That the written agreement of the parties dividing marital assets, debts and liabilities, a copy of which is filed with this petition, be incorporated into the final order and judgment of this Court granting the petition for dissolution of marriage.

C. (Optional) That ________________________________ be restored to her former/maiden name,
(Type or Print Wife's Name)
____.
(Type or Print Wife's Maiden OR Former Name)

D. That this Court grant the parties such other and further relief as may be just.

____________________________________ ____________________________________

Petitioner (signature) Respondent (signature)

VERIFICATION

STATE OF ILLINOIS)
) SS.
COUNTY OF ______________________________)

____, Petitioner, being first duly sworn upon oath, depose and
(Type or Print Plaintiff's Name)
say that I have read the foregoing Joint Petition for Simplified Dissolution of Marriage, understand the contents thereof, and believe the same to be true and correct to the best of my knowledge and belief.

____
Petitioner (signature)

Subscribed and sworn to before me, a Notary Public, this ______ day of ________________________, __________.

____
NOTARY PUBLIC

STATE OF ILLINOIS)
) SS.
COUNTY OF ______________________________)

____, Respondent, being first duly sworn upon oath, depose and
(Type or Print Defendant's Name)
say that I have read the foregoing Joint Petition for Simplified Dissolution of Marriage, understand the contents thereof, and believe the same to be true and correct to the best of my knowledge and belief.

____
Respondent (signature)

Subscribed and sworn to before me, a Notary Public, this ______ day of ________________________, __________.

____
NOTARY PUBLIC

IN THE CIRCUIT COURT OF THE ______________________ JUDICIAL
CIRCUIT, IN AND FOR ______________________ COUNTY, ILLINOIS

IN RE: The Marriage of

______________________________,
Petitioner,

and

No.______________

______________________________,
Respondent.

JOINT AFFIDAVIT REGARDING SEPARATION OF THE PARTIES
DIVISION OF PROPERTY AND WAIVER OF BIFURCATED HEARING

NOW COME ______________________, Petitioner, and ______________________,
(Type or Print Petitioner's Name) (Type or Print Respondent's Name)
Respondent, and being first sworn on their oaths, depose and state as follows:

1. That irreconcilable differences have caused the irretrievable breakdown of their marriage.

2. That all efforts at reconciliation of the differences between the parties have heretofore failed and future attempts at reconciliation would be impracticable and not in the best interest of the parties.

3. That the parties have lived separate and apart for a continuous period of more than six (6) months prior to the date of this affidavit, having separated on or about ______________, ________, ________, and having remained living separate for all times thereafter. (Month) (Day) (Year)

4. a. That each of the parties hereto expressly waive the requirement that the continuous period of living separate and apart be in excess of two (2) years in order for the Court to enter a Dissolution of Marriage based upon irreconcilable differences which have caused the irretrievable breakdown of their marriage; and,
   b. Each of the parties further stipulates that the requirement shall be reduced to a period only in excess of six (6) months rather than in excess of two (2) years as provided by Section 401(a) (2) of the Illinois Marriage and Dissolution of Marriage Act.

5. That the marital property belonging to the parties has been divided according to the terms of the written agreement of the parties filed with the Petition for Dissolution of Marriage in this cause, and that the parties have executed all documents required to carry out the agreement.

6. That the parties waive any right either may have to a bifurcated hearing in this cause.

7. That each of the parties represents that their signing of this Affidavit is their individual, sole, voluntary act.

____
Petitioner (signature)

Subscribed and sworn to this __________ day of
______________________, ________.

____
Notary Public

____
Respondent (signature)

Subscribed and sworn to this __________ day of
______________________, ________.

____
Notary Public

IN THE CIRCUIT COURT OF THE ______________________ JUDICIAL
CIRCUIT, IN AND FOR ______________________ COUNTY, ILLINOIS

IN RE: The Marriage of

______________________,
Petitioner,

and No.__________

______________________,
Respondent.

JUDGMENT FOR DISSOLUTION OF MARRIAGE

This cause having come on for hearing on the Joint Petition for Simplified Dissolution of marriage filed by the parties hereto; the Court having examined and considered the Petition, the Affidavit of the parties, and all other pleadings and exhibits filed in this matter; the Court having heard the testimony presented herein; and the Court being otherwise fully advised in the premises, finds as follows:

1. This Court has jurisdiction over the subject matter and the parties hereto.
2. ______________________ and/or ______________________ now, and for ninety
   (Type or Print Petitioner's Name and/or Respondent's Name, or Both Names)
   (90) days continuously and immediately preceding this date, have been residents of the State of Illinois.
3. The parties have been married for less than five (5) years prior to the filing of this petition; the parties were married on ______________________, __________; and the marriage was registered
   (Month) (Day) (Year)
   in ______________________ County, ______________________.
   (County)
4. The parties have lived separate and apart for a continuous period in excess of six (6) months; irreconcilable differences have caused the irretrievable breakdown of the marriage; efforts at reconciliation have failed; and, further efforts at reconciliation would not be in the best interests of the parties.
5. The parties have each signed an affidavit waiving the requirement for a continuous period living separate and apart in excess of two (2) years.
6. The parties have each signed a waiver of any right to a bifurcated hearing in this cause.
7. No children were born to or adopted by the parties during their relationship and to the best of her knowledge ______________________ is not pregnant at this time.
   (Type or Print Wife's Name)
8. Both the parties have waived any right to maintenance.
9. Neither party has any interest in real property. The parties have disclosed to each other all assets and their tax returns for all years of the marriage. The total annual income of the parties is less than $25,000.
10. The total fair market value of all marital property owned by the parties, after deducting all encumbrances, is less than $5,000.00. The parties have executed a written agreement, which the Court finds is not unconscionable, dividing all assets in excess of $100.00 in value and allocating responsibility for all debts and liabilities between the parties. A copy of the written agreement, signed by both parties, was filed with the petition in this cause and is hereby incorporated by reference as if fully set forth herein.

11. (Optional)____'s former/maiden name was
(Type or Print Wife's Name)

____.
(Type or Print Wife's Maiden OR Former Name)

WHEREFORE, IT IS HEREBY ORDERED, ADJUDGED AND DECREED:

A. The present marriage between the parties is hereby dissolved, and parties are each hereby awarded a Judgment of Dissolution of Marriage dissolving their present bonds of matrimony.

B. This Court adopts as a part of this Judgment, as if it were fully set forth herein, the agreement of the parties concerning the distribution of assets, debts and liabilities. Petitioner and Respondent each is hereby ordered to dispose of all claims each may have against the other , and to dispose of all assets, debts and liabilities, in accordance with and pursuant to the agreement entered into by the parties and presented to this Court. Petitioner and Respondent are each ordered to timely execute any and all titles, certificates and other documents of any kind or nature whatsoever, necessary to carry out the terms and condition of this Judgment of Dissolution of Marriage as to the division of assets, debts and liabilities ordered herein.

C. Each of the parties is hereby denied maintenance for now and for all times hereafter.

D. (Optional) ______________________________ is hereby restored to her former/maiden name,
(Type or Print Wife's Name)

____ .
(Type or Print Wife's Maiden OR Former Name)

E. Except for the provisions contained in this Judgment of Dissolution of Marriage, each of the parties is hereby barred and foreclosed from making any and all claims against the other whether for alimony or maintenance, homestead rights, dower rights, rights of inheritance or any and all other property rights, whether real, personal or mixed, which either of them may now have or may hereafter acquire arising out of the marital relationship heretofore existing between them.

F. This Court retains jurisdiction of this cause for the purpose of enforcing the provisions of this Judgment of Dissolution of Marriage.

ENTERED____________________________

APPROVED AS TO FORM AND CONTENT:

____
JUDGE

____
Petitioner (signature)

____
Respondent (signature)

IN THE CIRCUIT COURT OF THE ______________________ JUDICIAL
CIRCUIT, IN AND FOR ______________________ COUNTY, ILLINOIS

IN RE: The Marriage of

______________________________,
Petitioner,

and

No.______________

______________________________,
Respondent.

AGREEMENT AS TO ASSETS AND DEBTS

Now come ______________________________________, Petitioner, and
(Type or Print Petitioner's Name)
______________________________________ Respondent, and hereby agree
(Type or Print Respondent's Name)
to the following distribution of all marital assets in excess of One Hundred Dollars ($100.00) in value and the following division of all marital debts and liabilities.

Marital Assets

Description of Asset and Estimated Value (List all marital assets in excess of One Hundred Dollars [$100.00] in value - assets of lower value may be listed)	Party to Receive Asset (Enter name of Party [Husband or Wife] who will receive the asset)
1.______________________	______________________
2.______________________	______________________
3.______________________	______________________
4.______________________	______________________
5.______________________	______________________
6.______________________	______________________
7.______________________	______________________
8.______________________	______________________
9.______________________	______________________
10.______________________	______________________
11.______________________	______________________
12.______________________	______________________
13.______________________	______________________
14.______________________	______________________
15.______________________	______________________

Marital Debts and Liabilities

Description of Debt or Liability (List all Marital Debts and Liabilities)	Amount (List total balance due)	Account Number (List Account Number where applicable)	Party to Pay Debt (Enter name of Party [husband or wife] who will be responsible For paying the Debt or Liability)
1.________	$________	________	________
2.________	$________	________	________
3.________	$________	________	________
4.________	$________	________	________
5.________	$________	________	________
6.________	$________	________	________
7.________	$________	________	________
8.________	$________	________	________
9.________	$________	________	________
10.________	$________	________	________
11.________	$________	________	________
12.________	$________	________	________
13.________	$________	________	________
14.________	$________	________	________
15.________	$________	________	________

____

Petitioner's Signature

Subscribed and Sworn to before me this________

day of ____________________, ________.

____

Notary Public

(Seal)

____

Respondent's Signature

Subscribed and Sworn to before me this________

day of ____________________, ________.

____

Notary Public

(Seal)

IN THE CIRCUIT COURT OF THE ______________________ JUDICIAL
CIRCUIT, IN AND FOR ________________________ COUNTY, ILLINOIS

IN RE: The Marriage of

______________________________________,
Petitioner,

and

No.__________________

______________________________________,
Respondent.

PETITION FOR DISSOLUTION OF MARRIAGE

Now comes ______________________________, the Petitioner, and petitions this Court for dissolution of marriage and for other relief, and in support of said Petition, alleges as follows:

1. That the Petitioner is _____ years of age, presently residing in ___________________________, ___________________________, having resided in the State of Illinois since __________________, _______. That the Petitioner is employed at ____.

2. That the Respondent is _____ years of age, presently residing in ___________________________, ___________________________, having resided in the State of Illinois since __________________, _______. That the Respondent is employed at ____.

3. That the Petitioner and the Respondent were lawfully were married on ____________________,
(Month) (Day)

________, at ______________________________, ______________________________ County,
(Year) (City) (County)

______________________________________.
(State)

4. That the Petitioner is presently domiciled in the State of Illinois, and has been so domiciled for more than ninety (90) days prior to the filing of this Petition, thereby satisfying the jurisdictional requirements under Illinois law.

5. That the parties have lived separate and apart from each other continuously since ______________, ________, as evidenced by the Affidavits of the parties attached hereto and made a part hereof [COMPLETE ONLY IF GROUNDS WILL BE PARAGRAPH 6(b); IF PARAGRAPH 6(a) WILL BE USED, STRIKE OUT THIS ENTIRE PARAGRAPH].

6. [STRIKE OUT PARAGRAPH WHICH DOES NOT APPLY]

(a) That the Respondent, without cause or provocation by the Petitioner, has been guilty of extreme and repeated mental cruelty against the Petitioner.

(b) That irreconcilable differences have arisen during the course of the marriage which have caused an irretrievable breakdown of the marital relationship itself, and further, any future attempt at reconciliation by the parties would be impracticable and not in their best interests.

7. That there were ______ child(ren) born of the marriage, namely ______________________________ ____age(s) ______________________ respectively, and further, no children have been adopted by the parties/ ______________ child(ren) were adopted, namely ____, age(s) __________________________ respectively. ____ The wife is not now pregnant. ____ The wife is pregnant.

8. That the parties hereto have acquired certain debts and obligations during the course of their marriage, namely the following:

Creditor:	Amount:

9. That the parties hereto have acquired the following real property and personal property during the course of their marriage: ____ ____.

10. That the Petitioner, is a fit and proper person to the have the care, custody, control and education of the minor child(ren) of the parties, subject to reasonable visitation by the Respondent.

11. (Miscellaneous) ____ ____.

WHEREFORE, the Petitioner prays as follows:

1. That a Judgment for Dissolution of Marriage be entered in favor of both parties dissolving their marriage.

2. That the Petitioner be awarded the temporary and permanent care, custody, control and education of the minor child(ren) of the parties, subject to reasonable visitation by the Respondent.

3. That the Respondent be ordered to pay to the Clerk of Circuit Court of ______________________ County, Illinois, a reasonable sum of support, temporary and permanent, for the minor child(ren) until further order of the Court.

4. That the Court apportion and distribute the marital property of the parties, equitably and justly.

5. That allocation of the non-marital property of the parties be made by this Court.

6. That the Petitioner be awarded spousal maintenance, temporary and permanent.

7. That the Respondent be ordered to pay attorney's fees and costs incurred in this dissolution of marriage proceeding.

8. That the Petitioner have any other and further relief as the Court shall deem meet and just.

(IF NO CHILD SUPPORT OR ALIMONY REQUEST IS NEEDED,
STRIKE OUT PARAGRAPH 2, 3 AND/OR 6)

____

PETITIONER

STATE OF ILLINOIS)
) SS.
COUNTY OF)

____, being first duly sworn on oath, deposes and says that I am the Petitioner in the above entitled cause; that I have read the above and foregoing Petition for Dissolution of Marriage; that I have knowledge of the contents and facts thereof and that the statements contained therein are true and correct to the best of my knowledge and belief.

____

PETITIONER

Subscribed and sworn to before me this

_______day of ______________________, 19_____.

____

Notary Public

IN THE CIRCUIT COURT OF THE ____________________________ JUDICIAL
CIRCUIT, IN AND FOR ______________________________ COUNTY, ILLINOIS

IN RE: The Marriage of

____,
Petitioner,

and No.___________________

____,
Respondent.

FINANCIAL AFFIDAVIT

STATE OF ILLINOIS)
COUNTY OF)

BEFORE ME, this day personally appeared ____, who being duly sworn, deposes and says that the following information is true and correct according to his/her best knowledge and belief:

ITEM 1: EMPLOYMENT AND INCOME

OCCUPATION: ____
EMPLOYED BY: ____
ADDRESS: ____
____
SOC. SEC. #: ____
PAY PERIOD: ____
RATE OF PAY: ____

AVERAGE GROSS MONTHLY INCOME FROM EMPLOYMENT $____________

Bonuses, commissions, allowances, overtime, tips and similar payment ____________
Business Income from sources such as self-employment, partnership, close corporations, and/or independent contracts (gross receipts minus ordinary and necessary expenses required to produce income) ____________
Disability benefits ____________
Workers' Compensation ____________
Unemployment Compensation ____________
Pension, retirement, or annuity payments ____________
Social Security benefits ____________
Spousal support received from previous marriage ____________
Interest and dividends ____________
Rental income (gross receipts minus ordinary and necessary expenses required to produce income) ____________
Income from royalties, trust, or estates ____________

Reimbursed expenses and in kind payments to the extent that they reduce personal living expenses	________
Gains derived from dealing in property (not including nonrecurring gains)	________
Itemize any other income of a recurring nature	________
TOTAL MONTHLY INCOME	$________

LESS DEDUCTIONS:

Federal, state, and local income taxes (corrected for filing status and actual number of withholding allowances)	$________
FICA or self-employment tax (annualized)	________
Mandatory union dues	________
Mandatory retirement	________
Health insurance payments	________
Court ordered support payments for the children actually paid	________
TOTAL DEDUCTIONS	$________

ITEM 2: AVERAGE MONTHLY EXPENSES

HOUSEHOLD:

Mtg. or rent payments	________
Property taxes & insurance	________
Electricity	________
Water, garbage, & sewer	________
Telephone	________
Fuel oil or natural gas	________
Repairs and maintenance	________
Lawn and pool care	________
Pest control	________
Misc. household	________
Food and grocery items	________
Meals outside home	________
Other:	
________	________
________	________

AUTOMOBILE:

Gasoline and oil	________
Repairs	________
Auto tags and license	________
Insurance	________
Other:	
________	________
________	________

CHILDREN'S EXPENSES:

Nursery or baby-sitting	________
School tuition	________
School supplies	________
Lunch money	________
Allowance	________
Clothing	________
Medical, dental, prescriptions	________
Vitamins	________
Barber/beauty parlor	________
Cosmetics/toiletries	________
Gifts for special holidays	________
Other expenses:	
________	________
________	________

INSURANCES:

Health	________
Life	________
Other Insurance:	
________	________
________	________

OTHER EXPENSES NOT LISTED ABOVE:

Dry cleaning and laundry	________
Affiant's clothing	________
Affiant's medical, dental, prescriptions	________
Affiant's beauty salon/barber	________
Affiant's gifts (special holidays)	________
Pets:	
Grooming	________
Veterinarian	________
Membership Dues:	
Professional dues	________
Social dues	________
Entertainment	________
Vacations	________
Publications	________
Religious organizations	________
Charities	________
Miscellaneous	________

OTHER EXPENSES:

____________________	____________
____________________	____________
____________________	____________
____________________	____________

TOTAL ABOVE EXPENSES $____________

PAYMENTS TO CREDITORS:

TO WHOM:	BALANCE DUE:	MONTHLY PAYMENTS:

TOTAL MONTHLY PAYMENTS TO CREDITORS: $____________

TOTAL MONTHLY EXPENSES: $____________

ITEM 3: ASSETS (OWNERSHIP: IF JOINT, ALLOCATE EQUALLY)

Description	Value	Husband	Wife
Cash (on hand or in banks)			
Stocks/bonds/notes			
Real Estate:			
Home:			
Automobiles:			
Other personal property:			
Contents of home			
Jewelry			
Life ins./cash surrender value			
Other Assets:			
TOTAL ASSETS:	$	$	$

ITEM 4: LIABILITIES

Creditor	Security	Balance	Husband	Wife
________	________	________	________	________
________	________	________	________	________
________	________	________	________	________
________	________	________	________	________
________	________	________	________	________
________	________	________	________	________
________	________	________	________	________
________	________	________	________	________
________	________	________	________	________
________	________	________	________	________
TOTAL LIABILITIES:		$________	$________	$________

____
Affiant

Acknowledged before me on ______________ [date], by ______________ [name], who is personally known to me/ who produced ______________ [document] as identification, and who did take an oath.

____
NOTARY PUBLIC-STATE OF ILLINOIS/COURT CLERK

Name: ______________________
Commission No.: ______________________
My Commission Expires: ______________________

CERTIFICATE OF SERVICE

I CERTIFY that I have ____ mailed, ____ telefaxed and mailed, or ____ hand delivered a copy of the above Financial Affidavit to: ______________________________
____
______________________________[name and address].

____
Signature

IN THE CIRCUIT COURT OF THE ______________________ JUDICIAL
CIRCUIT, IN AND FOR ________________________ COUNTY, ILLINOIS

IN RE: The Marriage of

______________________________________,

Petitioner,

and   No.__________________

______________________________________,

Respondent.

RESPONSE TO PETITION FOR
DISSOLUTION OF MARRIAGE

Now comes the Respondent, ________________________________, appearing in his own behalf, and for his Response to the Petition for Dissolution of Marriage of the Petitioner, ________________________________, says as follows:

1. Admits the allegations contained in Paragraph One of said Petition.
2. Admits the allegations contained in Paragraph Two of said Petition.
3. Admits the allegations contained in Paragraph Three of said Petition.
4. Admits the allegations contained in Paragraph Four of said Petition.
5. Admits the allegations contained in Paragraph Five of said Petition
6. Denies the allegations contained in Paragraph Six (a) and Six (b) of said Petition.
7. Admits the allegations contained in Paragraph Seven of said Petition.
8. Admits the allegations contained in Paragraph Eight of said Petition.
9. Admits the allegations contained in Paragraph Nine of said Petition.
10. Admits the allegations contained in Paragraph Ten of said Petition.

WHEREFORE, Respondent prays that the Petition for Dissolution of Marriage of the Petitioner be dismissed at Petitioner's cost and for such other and further relief as the Court deems just and proper.

____
RESPONDENT

STATE OF ILLINOIS)
) SS.
COUNTY OF ____________________________)

____, being first duly sworn upon oath, deposes and states that I am the Respondent in the above entitled cause; that I have read the above and foregoing Response to Petition for Dissolution of Marriage, know the contents therein and that the statements contained therein are true and correct to the best of my knowledge and belief.

____

RESPONDENT

Subscribed and sworn to before me this

_______ day of ________________, ________.

____

Notary Public

IN THE CIRCUIT COURT OF THE _____________________ JUDICIAL
CIRCUIT, IN AND FOR ________________________ COUNTY, ILLINOIS

IN RE: The Marriage of

______________________________________,
Petitioner,

and No.________________

______________________________________,
Respondent.

AFFIDAVIT OF SEPARATION

I, ____, having been duly sworn upon oath, deposes and states as follows:

1. That I am the spouse of ____.

2. That we have lived separate and apart from each other since ________________________________, _______, due to the irreconcilable differences that have arisen during our marriage.

3. That said separation was voluntarily done on my part with our mutual consent.

Further Affiant sayeth not.

____
PETITIONER/RESPONDENT
(STRIKE OUT INAPPLICABLE
PARTY DESIGNATION)

Subscribed and sworn to before me this

_____ day of __________________, ______.

____
Notary Public

IN THE CIRCUIT COURT OF THE ______________________ JUDICIAL
CIRCUIT, IN AND FOR ________________________ COUNTY, ILLINOIS

IN RE: The Marriage of

_______________________________________,
Petitioner,

and No.__________________

_______________________________________,
Respondent.

STIPULATION
(IRRECONCILABLE DIFFERENCES)

IT IS HEREBY AGREED AND STIPULATED BY THE UNDERSIGNED PARTIES AS FOLLOWS:

That pursuant to a Petition for Dissolution of Marriage filed herein, ______________ ____, the Petitioner, and ____, the Respondent, hereby stipulate and agree to voluntarily and freely waive the requirement of separation for a period in excess of two (2) years and consent to the Court's entry of a Judgment for Dissolution of Marriage based upon our separation for a period of at least six (6) months prior to the entry of said Judgment.

That this Stipulation has been entered into after being fully advised of our rights pursuant to Chapter 40, Section 401(a)(2) of the Illinois Revised Statutes.

SO STIPULATED:

____
PETITIONER

____
RESPONDENT

IN THE CIRCUIT COURT OF THE ______________________ JUDICIAL CIRCUIT, IN AND FOR _______________________ COUNTY, ILLINOIS

IN RE: The Marriage of

_____________________________________,

Petitioner,

and

No.__________________

_____________________________________,

Respondent.

AFFIDAVIT AS TO MILITARY SERVICE

____ on oath states:

With respect to defendant

[ ] Defendant is

[ ] Defendant is not

[ ] Unable to determine if defendant is

in the military service of the United States.

The affidavit is based on these facts:

____

(Signed)

NAME ___________________________

ADDRESS ___________________________

____

CITY___________________________

TELEPHONE ______________________

Signed and sworn to before me

_____________________, __________

____

Notary Public

IN THE CIRCUIT COURT OF THE ______________________ JUDICIAL CIRCUIT, IN AND FOR ________________________ COUNTY, ILLINOIS

IN RE: The Marriage of

______________________________________,
Petitioner,

and

No.__________________

______________________________________,
Respondent.

CERTIFICATE OF MILITARY SERVICE

TO: U.S. Coast Guard Commander, GPIM-2, Locators, 2100 2nd St., S.W., Washington, DC 20593
AFMPC/RMIQL, Attn: Air Force Locator, Randolph AFB, TX 78150-6001
Department of Navy, Bureau of Navy Personnel, 2 Navy Annex, Washington, DC 20370-5000
CMC MMSB-10, HQ USMC, Bldg. 2008 Quantico, VA 22134-5002
Surgeon General, U.S. Public Health Service, Div. Of Comm., Off. Personnel, 5600 Fishers Lane, Rockville, MD 20857
Army World Wide Locator, U.S. Army Enlisted Records Center, Fort Benjamin Harrison, IN 46249-5601
Commander, U.S. Army Personnel Center, Officer Locator Branch, Attn: Locators, 200 Stovall Street, Alexandria, VA 22332

RE: __________________________________ __________________________
[Party] [Soc. Sec. #]

This case involves a dissolution of marriage. It is imperative that a determination be made whether the above named individual, who has an interest in these proceedings, is presently in the military service of the United States, and the date of induction and discharge, if any. This information is necessary to comply with Sec. 601 of the Soldier's and Sailor's Civil Relief Act of 1940, as amended. Please supply a certification of verification as soon as possible. My check is enclosed for your fees. Self-addressed stamped envelopes are enclosed.

DATED: __________________

____
Signature

Name ____________________________

Address __________________________

Telephone No. _____________________

IN THE CIRCUIT COURT OF THE ________________________ JUDICIAL CIRCUIT, IN AND FOR ________________________ COUNTY, ILLINOIS

IN RE: The Marriage of

____,
Petitioner,

and

No.____________________

____,
Respondent.

MOTION TO ENTER DEFAULT

TO THE CLERK OF COURT:

Please enter a default against Respondent who failed to respond to the petition.

DATED: ______________________

____
Signature

Name: ____________________________________
Address: __________________________________
Telephone: ________________________________

ORDER OF DEFAULT

A default is entered in this action against the Respondent for failure to serve or file a response or any paper as is required by law. Cause is continued for hearing and entry of Default Judgment to ___________________, ________, at __________ _____.M.

DATED: _________________

____
JUDGE

IN THE CIRCUIT COURT OF THE ______________________ JUDICIAL
CIRCUIT, IN AND FOR _______________________ COUNTY, ILLINOIS

IN RE: The Marriage of

______________________________________,
Petitioner,

and

No.__________________

______________________________________,
Respondent.

MARITAL SETTLEMENT AGREEMENT FOR DISSOLUTION OF MARRIAGE

We, ______________________________, and ______________________________, were married on ______________________. Because of difficulties in our marriage which are put forth as grounds for dissolution; we have made this agreement to settle once and for all the matters set forth below. Each of us states that nothing has been held back, that we have honestly included everything we could think of in listing the property that we own, that we have honestly disclosed out income to each other, and each of us states that we believe the other one has been open and honest in writing up this agreement. Each of us agrees to sign and exchange any papers that might be needed complete this agreement.

CHILD CUSTODY

[ ] *We will have joint legal custody; however, physical custody of the minor child(ren), ______________________________________ shall be awarded to the Husband; and the Wife shall have reasonable and liberal visitation rights.

[ ] *We will have joint legal custody; however, physical custody of the minor child(ren), ______________________________________ shall be awarded to the Wife; and the Husband shall have reasonable and liberal visitation rights.

[ ] Other:

* If a Joint Custody Agreement, a signed Joint Parenting Agreement is attached.

CHILD SUPPORT

[ ] The [ ] Husband [ ] Wife agrees to pay the sum of $_________ per __________ as support and maintenance for the minor child(ren) in the physical custody of the other parent. Child support shall be adjusted, according to the then existing child support guidelines, upon the occurrence of any of the following events: a child becoming 18 years of age and emancipated, including graduation from high school; the death of a child; or a legal change in custody.

[ ] The [ ] Husband [ ] Wife agrees to maintain health insurance coverage for the minor child/children as long as such insurance is available at a reasonable group rate.

[ ] Other (include agreement on claiming children for tax exemptions):

DIVISION OF PROPERTY

We shall each keep our own personal clothing and effects, unless otherwise indicated below. We divide our property as follows:

1. Husband transfers to Wife as her sole and separate property:
   A.
   B.
   C.
   D.
   E.
   F.
   G.
   [ ] Continued on Additional Sheet.
2. Wife transfers to Husband as his sole and separate property:
   A.
   B.
   C.
   D.
   E.
   F.
   G.
   [ ] Continued on Additional Sheet.

DIVISION OF DEBTS

We shall each be responsible for our own after-separation debts unless otherwise indicated below. We divide responsibility for payment of our debts as follows:

3. Husband shall pay the following debts and will hold Wife harmless upon them:
   A.
   B.
   C.
   D.
   E.
   F.
   G.
   [ ] Continued on Additional Sheet.

4. Wife shall pay the following debts and will hold Husband harmless upon them:
   A.
   B.
   C.
   D.
   E.
   F.
   G.
   [ ] Continued on Additional Sheet.

ALIMONY

[ ] No alimony shall be awarded to either party.
[ ] The [ ] Husband [ ] Wife shall pay alimony to the other party in the sum of $__________ per ___________, for a period of ____________________________________; or until the [ ] Husband [ ] Wife dies or remarries, whichever occurs first.

ATTORNEY FEES (IF APPLICABLE):

DATED: ______________________

____
Wife's signature

Name ____________________________
Address____________________________
____

Telephone No. ____________________

SWORN TO and signed before me
on ______________________, ________.

____
NOTARY PUBLIC
My commission expires:

DATED: ______________________

____
Husband's signature

Name ____________________________
Address ____________________________
____

Telephone No. ____________________

SWORN TO and signed before me
on ______________________, ________.

____
NOTARY PUBLIC
My commission expires:

IN THE CIRCUIT COURT OF THE ______________________ JUDICIAL
CIRCUIT, IN AND FOR ______________________ COUNTY, ILLINOIS

IN RE: The Marriage of

______________________________________,
Petitioner,

and No.________________

______________________________________,
Respondent.

JUDGMENT OF DISSOLUTION OF MARRIAGE

This action was heard before the Court. On the evidence presented,

IT IS ADJUDGED that the bonds of marriage between the Husband, ____________ ____________________ and the Wife,____________________________, are dissolved.

IT IS FURTHER ADJUDGED that:

[ ] 1. The settlement agreement between the parties filed in this action was executed voluntarily after full disclosure and is approved and incorporated in this judgment by reference, and the parties are ordered to comply with it.

[ ] 2. The Wife's former name is restored and she shall hereafter be known as:

____.

[ ] 3. The parties shall share parenting responsibilities; however, physical custody of the minor child(ren) of the parties shall be awarded to the party designated below:

Name of Child — Child's Birthdate — Custody Awarded To:

Each party shall have the right to visit any child not in his or her custody at reasonable times and places after reasonable notice to the custodial party.

[ ] 4. The [ ] Husband [ ] Wife shall pay child support to the other party in the sum of $_____________ per _____________,beginning _______________, ________. Said support shall be reduced according to the then existing child support guidelines when each child reaches 18 year of age; and emancipated (including graduation from high school), marries, or dies, whichever occurs first.

[ ] 5. The [ ] Husband [ ] Wife shall provide health insurance coverage for the minor child(ren) whenever such insurance is reasonably available.

[ ] 6. The [ ] Husband [ ] Wife shall pay alimony to the other party in the sum of $___________ per ____________, beginning ___________________________, ________, to terminate:

[ ] On ____________________, ________, or on the death or remarriage of said other party, whichever occurs first.

[ ] Upon the death or remarriage of the other party.

[ ] Alimony is [ ] Awarded [ ] Not Awarded pursuant to the request and agreement of the parties.

[ ] Alimony is [ ] Awarded [ ] Not Awarded based upon the following reasons:

[ ] 7. The Husband shall transfer to the Wife as her sole and separate property:

[ ] 8. The Wife shall transfer to the Husband as his sole and separate property:

[ ] 9. The Husband shall pay the following debts and shall not at any time hold the Wife responsible for them:

[ ] 10. The Wife shall pay the following debts and shall not at any time hold the Husband responsible for them:

[ ] 11. The parties' nonmarital assets and debts shall be distributed as follows:

HUSBAND'S	WIFE'S

[ ] 12. Other Provisions (including special distribution of nonmarital property, tax exemptions and attorney fees):

SO ORDERED,

DATED: ______________________ ____________________________________

JUDGE

NOTICE TO WITHHOLD INCOME FOR CHILD SUPPORT

State of Illinois
Co./City/Dist. of ____________________

Date of Order/Notice ____________________

Court/Case Number ____________________

_______ Original Order/Notice
_______ Amended Order/Notice
_______ Terminate Order/Notice

____________________ Employer/Withholder's Federal EIN Number	) Re:	____________________ Employee/Obligor's Name (Last/First/MI)
____________________ Employer/Withholder's Name	)	____________________ Employee/Obligor's Social Security No.
____________________ Employer/Withholder's Address	)	
____________________	)	
____________________	)	
____________________	)	____________________ Custodial Parent's Name (Last/First/MI)
Child(ren)'s Name(s): DOB:		**Child(ren)'s Name(s): DOB:**

ORDER INFORMATION: This is a Notice to Withhold Income for Child Support based upon an order for support from ____________. By law you are required to deduct these amounts from the above-named employee's/obligor's income until ____________ even if the Notice is not issued by your State. *See important information Employer Summary Notice.

____ If checked, you are required to enroll the child(ren) identified above in any health insurance coverage available through the employee's/obligor's employment. ____________________

$__________ per ____________ in current support
$__________ per ____________ in past-due support totaling $__________ Arrears 12 weeks or greater? Yes/No
$__________ per ____________ in medical support
$__________ per ____________ in other (specify) ____________________
$__________ per ____________ in other (specify) ____________________
for a total of $______________ per ____________ to be forwarded to the payee below.

You do not have to vary your pay cycle to be in compliance with the support order. If your pay cycle does not match the ordered support payment cycle, use the following to determine how much to withhold:
$________ per weekly pay period. $________ per semimonthly pay period (twice a month)
$________ per biweekly pay period (every 2 weeks) $________ per monthly pay period.

REMITTANCE INFORMATION: Follow the laws and procedures of the employee's/obligor's principal place of employment even if such laws and procedures are different from this paragraph:
You must begin withholding no later than the first pay period occurring 14 working days after the date of this Order/Notice. Send payments within seven (7) working days of the paydate/date of withholding. You are entitled to deduct a fee of your actual cost not to exceed $5 monthly to defray the cost of withholding.

When remitting payment provide the paydate/date of withholding and the Court/Case Number and employee name.

Make it payable to : ____________________

Send check to: ____________________

____

____

Authorized by: ____________________

IN THE CIRCUIT COURT OF THE ______________________ JUDICIAL
CIRCUIT, IN AND FOR ________________________ COUNTY, ILLINOIS

IN RE: The Marriage of

____________________________________,
Petitioner,

and

No.__________________

____________________________________,
Respondent.

SUBPOENA DUCES TECUM

To: ______________________________,

YOU ARE HEREBY COMMANDED PERSONALLY to be and appear before the ____________________ Judicial Circuit, ____________________County Court House (____________________, Illinois), in Court Room _______, on ______________________, ________, at __________ A.M./P.M. and produce at the time and place aforesaid, and to bring to be used as evidence, certain instruments of writing purporting to be:

and then and there to testify, and the truth to speak concerning those things of which you may have knowledge, and the import of such instruments of writing concerning the above captioned case now pending and undetermined in the ____________________ JUDICIAL CIRCUIT, on the part of ____.

YOUR FAILURE TO COMPLY WITH THIS SUBPOENA CAN SUBJECT YOU TO PUNISHMENT FOR CONTEMPT OF COURT.

WITNESS: ____________________________, CLERK OF SAID COURT AND THE SEAL THEREOF AT HIS OFFICE, IN SAID COUNTY OF THIS _______ DAY OF ______________________, __________

(SEAL OF
COURT)

____
Clerk

NAME ________________________
ADDRESS ______________________
____
TELEPHONE ____________________

NOTICE TO WITNESS

The party who has requested this subpoena is listed herein. Any questions regarding your knowledge of the subject matter or testimony in the case should be directed to him/her.
DO NOT CALL THE CIRCUIT COURT CLERK.

______________________ - ______________________ COUNTY CIRCUIT CLERK
______________________, ILLINOIS

IN THE CIRCUIT COURT OF THE ______________________ JUDICIAL
CIRCUIT, IN AND FOR ________________________ COUNTY, ILLINOIS

IN RE: The Marriage of

_______________________________________,
Petitioner,

and No.________________

_______________________________________,
Respondent.

AFFIDAVIT FOR SERVICE BY PUBLICATION

____ on oath states:

1. Defendant* ____.

2. Defendant's place of residence** ____
____.

____
Signature

Signed and sworn to before me on

__________________________, __________

____
Notary Public

Name ______________________________
Address ____________________________
City _______________________________
Telephone __________________________

* Insert one of the following:
1. resides outside the state
2. has gone out of the state
3. on due inquiry cannot be found so that process cannot be served upon him
4. is concealed within the state so that process cannot be served upon him

**Insert one of the following:
1. is
2. upon diligent inquiry cannot be ascertained and his last known place of residence is

IN THE CIRCUIT COURT OF THE ______________________ JUDICIAL
CIRCUIT, IN AND FOR ________________________ COUNTY, ILLINOIS

IN RE: The Marriage of

_____________________________________,

Petitioner,

and

No.__________________

_____________________________________,

Respondent.

NOTICE BY PUBLICATION

The requisite affidavit for publication having been filed, NOTICE IS HEREBY GIVEN YOU, _______________________, respondent, that this case has been commenced in this court by the petitioner against you for dissolution of marriage and other relief.

UNLESS YOU file your answer or otherwise file your appearance in this case in the office of the clerk of this court, Room _______ in the ____________ County Courthouse, _________________________, Illinois, on or before ____________________, _______, * A JUDGMENT OR DECREE BY DEFAULT MAY BE TAKEN AGAINST YOU FOR THE RELIEF ASKED IN THE COMPLAINT.

____

________________ County Circuit Clerk

____

Petitioner

____

Address

____

City

____

Telephone

*Not less than 30 days from the first date of publication. Must be published three (3) times. (2-207 Code of Civil Procedure)

Dear Sir or Madam:

Enclosed is a Notice by Publication as required by law, to be published three times.

Please take notice of the return date in the Notice of Action, and ensure that the dates of publication meet the legal requirement that the return date be "not less than thirty (30) days after the first publication." If you cannot comply with this requirement, please notify me immediately so I can obtain an amended Notice by Publication.

Thank you for your attention to this matter.

Sincerely,

IN THE CIRCUIT COURT OF THE ______________________ JUDICIAL
CIRCUIT, IN AND FOR ______________________ COUNTY, ILLINOIS

IN RE: The Marriage of

No. ______________

[ ] Order application to (sue)(defend) as a poor person is granted.

____
Petitioner,

[ ] Order application to (sue)(defend) as a poor person is denied.

and

____
Respondent.

Date______________________
Enter______________________
Judge

APPLICATION TO SUE OR DEFEND AS A POOR PERSON

I, ____

[ ] on my own behalf
[ ] as [ ] Parent [ ] Guardian [ ] Other ______________________ of
______________________________, a ______________________
(Name) (Minor)(Incompetent)

1. Applicant's occupation or means of subsistence:
   A. Applicant is employed as ______________________ (Job)
   by ______________________ (Employer)
   B. Applicant's other sources of income or support are:
   ____
2. Applicant's income for the preceding year was $______________.
3. The sources and amount of income expected by the applicant hereafter are:
   ____
   The person dependent on applicant for support are:
4. Applicant owns (A) no real estate except: (Location and Value)
   ____ and
   (B) Personal Property which in the aggregate does not exceed $ ______________
   and consists of:______________________________
   including a ______________ motor vehicle, valued at $______________.
5. No applications were filed by or on behalf of application for leave to sue or defend as a poor person during the preceding year except:
6. Applicant is unable to pay the costs of this case.
7. Applicant has a meritorious [ ] Claim [ ] Defense

Subscribed and sworn before me
Date: ______________________

____
Notary Public - Circuit Court Clerk

____
Signature of Applicant

Name: ______________________

Address: ______________________

City: ______________________

Phone: ______________________

CLERK OF THE ______________ JUDICIAL CIRCUIT COURT

IN THE CIRCUIT COURT OF THE ______________________ JUDICIAL
CIRCUIT, IN AND FOR ________________________ COUNTY, ILLINOIS

IN RE: The Marriage of

______________________________________,

Petitioner,

and

No.__________________

______________________________________,

Respondent.

PETITION FOR TEMPORARY RELIEF

Now comes the Petitioner, ________________________________, and for his/her Petition for Temporary Relief, states as follows:

1. That he/she is the Petitioner/Respondent in the above entitled cause.

2. a) That the parties have ________ minor children, currently residing with the Petitioner/Respondent, and the requesting party herein has insufficient funds to support the minor child(ren) [child support request - strike out if does not apply].

b) The Petitioner/Respondent is without sufficient funds to support him-self/herself during the pendency of this cause [maintenance request - strike out if does not apply].

3. That the opposing party is able bodied, employed and well able to contribute to the support of the Petitioner/Respondent/the minor child(ren) of the parties.

WHEREFORE, the Petitioner/Respondent prays that this Court enter an Order granting temporary child support and/or temporary maintenance during the pendency of these proceedings, and for such other and further relief as the Court deems just and proper.

____

PETITIONER/RESPONDENT
(STRIKE OUT INAPPLICABLE PARTY DESIGNATION)

STATE OF ILLINOIS)
) SS.
COUNTY OF ____________________)

____, being first duly sworn upon his/her oath, deposes and says that he/she is the Petitioner/Respondent in the above entitled cause; that he/she has read the above and foregoing Petition for Temporary Relief by him/her subscribed; knows the contents therein and that the statements contained therein are true and correct to the best of his/her knowledge and belief.

____
PETITIONER/RESPONDENT
(STRIKE OUT INAPPLICABLE PARTY DESIGNATION)

Subscribed and sworn to before me this

_____ day of ________________, ______.

____
Notary Public

[STRIKE OUT ALL INAPPLICABLE PORTIONS OF THIS FORM, INCLUDING PARTY DESIGNATION AND REQUEST FOR CHILD SUPPORT IF NO CHILDREN OF THE PARTIES AND MAINTENANCE IF ONLY CHILD SUPPORT IS REQUESTED]

IN THE CIRCUIT COURT OF THE ______________________ JUDICIAL
CIRCUIT, IN AND FOR ________________________ COUNTY, ILLINOIS

IN RE: The Marriage of

_______________________________________,
Petitioner,

and

No.__________________

_______________________________________,
Respondent.

ORDER FOR TEMPORARY SUPPORT AND CUSTODY

Upon consideration of the petitioner's motion, and the Court being fully advised in the premises;

IT IS ORDERED that:

[ ] Temporary custody of the minor child(ren) of the parties shall be awarded to the petitioner, and the respondent shall have reasonable visitation rights.

[ ] The respondent shall pay the sum of $___________ per __________ for the temporary support of the minor child(ren).

[ ] The respondent shall pay the sum of $___________ per ______________ as temporary alimony to the petitioner.

All sums to be paid pursuant to this order shall be paid through the clerk of the court, by way of an order for withholding.

This order shall remain in effect until the entry of the final judgment of dissolution of marriage, or until further order of this Court.

ORDERED in ______________________________, Illinois, on this ________ day of

_____________________________, 19____.

____
Circuit Judge

INDEX